Contents

Editor's Introduction: Studying Leisure Cultures, Consumption and Commodification

John Horne

University of Edinburgh

Introduction

This volume is one of three to result from the conference "Leisure: Centres and Peripheries", or "LSA 2000", the 25th Annual Conference of the Leisure Studies Association, hosted by Glasgow Caledonian University in July 2000. The 130 delegates heard 84 papers that offered a variety of approaches to and perspectives on the changing social, political and economic context of different forms of leisure. Contributors to the conference reflected both the multi-disciplinarity of leisure studies as a field and the multi-cultural composition of leisure studies scholarship.

The focus of this volume is on studies of the consumption and commodification of leisure. The papers are grouped into two parts. Part One deals with the diffusion, transformation and contestation of change in the consumption of a variety of leisure forms, including sport, the arts and cultural recreations. The papers in Part Two provide views of developments in place marketing, the invention of tradition and the leisure experience in one of the most commodified forms of leisure, tourism. Underlying these two parts and the collection as a whole are two themes that the rest of this introduction will outline.

Consumption and commodification

> The general thesis suggested by the sociological study of consumer behaviour is that consumption is the expressive aspect of style of life, and that style of life has developed a much greater significance as a mode of organising individual behaviour and leisure, careers and, therefore as a form of social structure. (Burns, 1966: p. 322)

Despite its early consideration by Tom Burns the academic study of consumption has only taken off in the past decade. Tomlinson (1990), Featherstone (1991), Lee (1993,

2000), Miller (1995), Nava *et al.* (1997), Slater (1997a and 1997b) and Edwards (2000) are just a few of the publications reflecting this growth. The word has increasingly crept into leisure studies conferences and publications (Merkel *et al.*, 1998; Whannel, 2000). It is perhaps not surprising, when we consider how many aspects of modern consumption relate to leisure (see Figure 1), that some have argued that consumption studies may even pose a threat to leisure studies (Roberts, 1997).

Figure 1   *16 Features of modern consumption*   (source: Lury, 1996: pp. 29–36)

- the widespread availability of consumer goods
- the marketization (privatization?) of services
- the popularity of shopping as leisure
- growth in different forms of shopping
- political organization of consumers
- increased visibility of the consumption of sport and leisure
- widespread availability of credit, and potential for debt
- increase in sites for purchase and consumption — the mall
- increase in packaging and promotion of consumer goods
- pervasiveness of advertising in everyday life
- increased emphasis on style, design and appearance of goods
- manipulation of time and space in the promotion of products
- the emergence of consumer crimes
- the impossibility of avoiding making choices about goods
- increased visibility of consumer illnesses / addictions
- interest in the personal and collective collection.

It was Ken Roberts (1997: p 369) who suggested that "old questions are the right response to new challenges" in the sociological study of leisure. Sociology has asked five basic questions: how much leisure do people have; how might people use it; how do people actually use leisure; why do they behave in this way; and what are the consequences of leisure behaviour in relation to social class, age, ethnicity and gender divisions? He argued that the sociology of leisure had accomplished many of the tasks set out for it, but that its success needed to be tempered by recognition of its limitations. Each of the questions identified by Roberts with respect to the study of leisure were, he argued, broadly consistent with those found in the study of consumption — "how much does the population consume, how is consumption distributed, which differences are due to opportunity and which to desire, and what are the consequences of different levels and types of consumption?" (Roberts, 1997: p. 375). Yet Roberts did not provide a clear definition of the difference between them since he wrote that leisure was both broader and narrower than consumption (Roberts, 1997: p. 376).

Another commentator on the rise of consumption studies, or the "new materialism" as David Chaney (1998) refers to it, suggests that the growth of interest in consumption has been underpinned by three developments. Firstly, shifting notions of the balance between citizenship and consumerism, or between the state and the market, in social, cultural, and therefore, as well, leisure, policy. Secondly, attacks on the foundational models of social science, especially the notion that the history of modernity was the history of developments in productive forces, as opposed to consumption. Thirdly, and related to the second point, was the impact of the "new materialism" on the concepts used to analyse aspects of social formations. One feature of this shift evident in leisure studies was the argument over " lifestyle" as a competitor concept to social class (Veal, 1989, 1993).

In assessing the importance of consumption perhaps food is an obvious place to start. Stephen Mennell (1985) suggested that the history of food in Britain demonstrated the diminishing of contrasts and the increase in varieties of food consumed. Mennell (1985: p. 322) argued that "diminishing contrasts/increasing varieties" was "one trend, not two: for in spite of the apparent contradiction between diminishing contrasts and increasing varieties, these are both facets of the same processes". However, the use of the "diminishing contrasts/increasing varieties" thesis, derived from Norbert Elias (1982), is problematic. In a sustained critique Alan Warde (1997: p. 166) has shown how it was a theoretically dubious, causally indeterminate and empirically suspect notion. Just like the other figurational conception, "the civilising process", which is able to move in both a "civilising" and "de-civilising" direction, it is difficult to discern from the "diminishing contrasts/increasing varieties" phrase which phenomena exhibit diminishing difference and which are undergoing diversification. As Warde (1997: p. 28) noted, "without some clear distinction between the two categories of process, between contrasts and variations, the neat phrase merely says that some phenomena become less diverse, others more diverse". Warde has shown that increasing variation in the consumption of food, the availability of new products and new channels of communication about food are best understood in relation to the outcomes of capitalist industrial activity. Warde concluded that the "mechanism that best explains Mennell's description of the 20th century is commodification" (Warde, 1997: p. 171). If a much more consistent explanation for changes in consumption patterns of food in Britain in the twentieth century is increasing commodification, it may be that we need to return to some old questions, but not necessarily the same ones that Roberts, from a socio-cultural pluralist perspective on leisure, would focus on.

Over 130 years ago Marx deliberately began *Capital* Volume 1 with a chapter on commodities. The opening sentence indicated why:

> The wealth of societies in which the capitalist mode of production prevails appears as an 'immense collection of commodities. (Marx, 1976/1867: p. 125)

Capitalism is an economic system in which the commodity — something whose value is defined in monetary terms and which is produced to be sold — becomes a universal, taken for granted, natural phenomenon, rather than a historically novel and specific feature of a particular way of organising the production of goods and services. Consumer culture "is essentially the culture of a market society, one in which needs are mediated by the exchange of commodities" (Slater, 1997b: p. 53).

It was C. Wright Mills (1951: p. 237) who acerbically noted the consequences of this for leisure when he wrote that: "Each day men sell little pieces of themselves in order to try to buy them back each night and week end with the coin of 'fun'". In his latest book on leisure, Roberts (1999) suggests that Mills's view reduces leisure to consumption. Instead, Roberts argues that there is a great amount of non-commodified leisure and hence that leisure is broader than consumption. Roberts is equivocal about adopting the more extreme view that consumption has become "the vanguard of history" (Miller, 1995: p. 1). Roberts does not accept this last position, since he recognises there are instances in leisure where commodification is a problem.

Sport is the most notable area of leisure that has until recently been insulated from the influence of the market economy. As the journalist and writer Hunter Davies once noted, "Every year United fans have their ashes scattered on the turf at Old Trafford. How often do you see that happening at Tesco's?" (quoted in Miles, 1998: p. 130).

For most of the 20th century, sport was conceived of as a form of culture outside the social relations of capitalist consumer culture. In the last twenty years this isolation has broken up. A transformation of sport has occurred via the "unholy alliance" of sport, media and advertising (Whannel, 1986; 1992 Horne *et al.*, 1999). Brick and Morrow, in this volume, consider the consequences of this in different ways in their papers.

Television has been "the single most influential driving force underlying the commodification of sport" (Miles, 1998: p. 140). If we ask what caused the increased media interest in sports programming? We begin to see a different picture emerge than one of consumer driven production. It was not simply due to either greater free time or the sudden growth of widespread interest in sport. Increasing commercial pressures on television companies, the cost benefits of sport vis-à-vis other TV shows (drama, documentaries, etc.) and the development of new, and competing, media (video, cable, satellite, digital, internet, mobile phones) have all been responsible for the search for relatively low cost means of attracting or maintaining audiences.

Sport has played a significant role in developments in television that have occurred since the spread of neo-liberal policies in the 1980s. These developments have included the limitation of cross-media ownership regulations, the reduction of public sector broadcasting budgets, the opening up of terrestrial TV to international capital, and criticism of public service broadcasting as elitist and inefficient. Sport has been central to these developments since it provides relatively cheap content for filling hours of TV and is attractive enough to some viewers to entice them to new technologies, like digital TV. Rupert Murdoch's News International Corporation devoted more energy to dominating global television sport in the 1990s than any of the other leading media corporations. As mediated events, football, and other sports, have been used as a 'battering ram' by Murdoch as part of commercial strategies of consolidation and horizontal integration.

Hence commodification is supported by various kinds of techniques to shape the market. As Raymond Williams (1980: p. 186) pointed out:

> In the production of goods for personal use, the critical problem posed by the factory of advanced machines was that of the organization of the market. The modern factory requires not only smooth and steady distributive channels ... but also definite indications of demand without which the expensive processes of capitalisation and equipment would be too great a risk ... Modern advertising ... is one of the most important of these devices, and it is perfectly true to say that modern capitalism could not function without it.

The contemporary period of consumer culture, in which discourses of 'variety' and 'choice' have been dominant, can be seen as the product of this apparatus of the organization of consumer demand. As Williams, again, noted, "The system of organized magic, which is modern advertising, is primarily important as a functional obscuring of (this) choice" (Williams, 1980: p. 186).

Despite this critique it can be agreed with Roberts that taste in leisure, as in foodstuffs and other cultural activities, is slow to change and continuities prevail. Without detailed empirical research tastes for leisure and cultural pursuits and the way people engage with such activities remain obscure. Equally, however, the impact on sports and leisure culture generally of new mass communications technology — including satellite and digital TV, the availability of sports information and chat lines on the internet, sports video games and phone-in sports radio programmes — are recent developments in need of empirical enquiry. Bryce provides a start to this in her paper on the technological transformation of leisure.

Commodification refers to both "the making into a commodity for sale on the marketplace of items or services which were previously not part of market logic" and "the process by which people and things acquire value, which enables them to be exchanged for profit" (Miller *et al.*, 2001: p. 130). Gray looks at the political dimensions of this with respect to the arts in his paper.

Developments in sport and leisure need to be understood in the context of specific political, economic and ideological conjunctures. The mass media have become increasingly central to the production and circulation of the sociocultural meanings of sport and leisure cultures in contemporary society. Jackson's paper considers sport and leisure long before TV, but utilises the newspaper press as a means to obtain information about leisure in early nineteenth century Scotland.

Lury and Warde (1997: p. 101) have noted that in studying consumption some social scientists have begun "adopting a view of general social practice that reflects the models of the consumer current in advertising practice". Decision-making is "conceived as following the logic of the shopper rather than of moral agent, citizen, associate, or whoever" (Lury and Warde, 1997: p. 101). In this respect consumer behaviour has been placed "at the very centre of the organization of everyday life" (Lury and Warde, 1997: p. 101). None of the studies in this volume adopt such a simplistic model of the leisure consumer. Instead they point to the need to recognise the links between the growth of interest in consumption with developments in consumerism and citizenship.

Each paper in this volume offers a different vantage point from which to consider recent developments in leisure. Whilst the papers in both parts reflect a higher than usual focus on leisure issues in Scotland and Scottish case studies, the underlying themes identified by the authors are much more widely applicable to the understanding of contemporary processes affecting the development of leisure. Hence, as Jackson amongst others notes, this volume also demonstrates the role of studies of the periphery in generating fresh insight into the central concerns of the field.

References

Burns, T. (1966) 'The study of consumer behaviour: a sociological view', *Archives Europeenes de Sociologie* Vol. VII: pp. 313–329.

Chaney, D. (1998) 'The new materialism? The challenge of consumption', *Work, Employment and Society* Vol. 12, No. 3: pp. 533–544.

Edwards, T. (2000) *Contradictions of consumption.* Buckingham: Open University Press.

Elias, N. (1982) *State formation and civilisation.* Oxford: Blackwell.

Featherstone, M. (1991) *Consumer culture and postmodernism*. London: Sage.

Horne, J., Tomlinson, A. and Whannel, G. (1999) *Understanding sport: An introduction to the sociological and cultural analysis of sport*. London: E. and F.N. Spon.

Lee, M. (ed) (2000) *The consumer society reader*. Oxford: Blackwell.

——— (1993) *Consumer culture reborn*. London: Routledge.

Lury, C. (1996) *Consumer culture*. Cambridge: Polity.

Lury, C. and Warde, A. (1997) 'Investments in the imaginary consumer: Conjectures regarding power, knowledge and advertising', in M. Nava *et al.* (eds) *Buy this book: Studies in advertising and consumption*. London: Routledge, pp. 87–102.

Marx, K. (1976/1867) *Capital, Volume One*. Harmondsworth: Penguin.

Mennell, S. (1985) *All manners of food*. Oxford: Blackwell.

Merkel, U., Lines, G. and McDonald, I. (1998) *The production and consumption of sport cultures: Leisure, culture and commerce* (LSA Publication No. 62). Eastbourne: Leisure Studies Association.

Miller, D. (ed) (1995) *Acknowledging consumption*. London: Routledge.

Miller, T., Lawrence, G., McKay, J. and Rowe, D. (2001) *Globalization and sport*. London: Sage.

Miles, S. (1998) *Consumerism: As a way of life*. London: Sage.

Mills, C. W. (1951) *White collar*. New York: Oxford University Press.

——— (1959) *The sociological imagination*. New York: Oxford University Press.

Morrow, S. (1999) *The new business of football*. London: Macmillan.

Nava, M., Blake, A., MacRury, I and Richards, B. (eds) (1997) *Buy this book: Studies in advertising and consumption*. London: Routledge.

Roberts, K. (1997) 'Why old questions are the right response to new challenges: the sociology of leisure in the 1990s', *Society and Leisure* Vol. 20, No. 2: pp. 369–381.

——— (1999) *Leisure in contemporary society*. Oxford: CABI.

Slater, D. (1997a) *Consumer culture and modernity*. Cambridge: Polity.

——— (1997b) 'Consumer culture and the politics of need', in Nava, M., *et al.* (eds) *Buy this book: Studies in advertising and consumption*. London: Routledge, pp. 51–63.

Tomlinson, A. (ed) (1990) *Consumption, identity and style*. London: Routledge.

Warde, A. (1997) *Consumption, food and taste*. London: Sage.

Whannel, G. (1986) 'The unholy alliance: Notes on television and the re-making of British sport', *Leisure Studies* Vol. 5, No. 1: pp. 22–37.

——— (1992) *Fields in vision*. London: Routledge.

Whannel, G. (ed) (2000) *Consumption and participation: Leisure, culture and commerce* (LSA Publication No. 64). Eastbourne: Leisure Studies Association.

Williams, R. (1980) *Problems in materialism and culture*. London: Verso.

——— (1977) *Marxism and literature*. Oxford: Oxford University Press.

——— (1961) *The long revolution*. Harmondsworth: Penguin.

About the Contributors

Carlton Brick is Post-Doctoral Research Fellow in Social and Cultural Studies in Sport and Leisure at the University of Surrey Roehampton. He has published widely on such issues as commodification, regulation and the cultural politics of contemporary football. He is a founding member of the football supporters civil rights campaign, 'Libero', and is editor of the fanzine, 'Offence'.

Jo Bryce is currently a lecturer in Psychology at the University of Central Lancashire, Preston (UK). Her research focuses on a number of interconnected areas relating to technology and society, as well as organisational psychology/. Currently her research focuses on investigating the psychological and social aspects of computer gaming, the relationship between technological develop and changing leisure practices, and the organisational aspects of the computer gaming industry. A number of conferences and journal papers have resulted from these interests. Her PhD research focused on an evaluation of models of the relationship between work, leisure and psychological well-being, with a particular focus on the gender dynamics of this relationship. She is currently a member of the World Leisure Commission on Youth and Society, and Co-Director of the Digiplay Initiative.

MariaLaura Di Domenico is at present undertaking research at the University of Strathclyde for a PhD on small-scale hospitality providers in the cities of Dundee and Inverness. This reflects her research interests in entrepreneurship and small businesses in the hospitality/tourism sector, and in urban tourism and urban identities. The latter interests, as well as her other research interest in industrial heritage tourism, are reflected in the research work which she undertook in Dundee for her recently completed MRes in Scottish Studies when she was based at the Research Centre for Scottish Studies also at the University of Strathclyde. She still teaches Scottish Studies there on a part-time basis, and is also a part-time lecturer in tourism at the University of Abertay Dundee.

Clive Gray is Principal Lecturer in Politics and Public Administration at De Montfort University, Leicester. He is the author of *Government Beyond the Centre* (Macmillan, 1994), and *The Politics of the Arts in Britain* (Macmillan, 2000), as well as many articles on decentralised politics, comparative public policy and the politics of the arts. His current research concerns arts policies at the local and regional levels in Britain and Europe.

Euan Hague is a Post-Doctoral Research Associate at Syracuse University, New York, where he teaches Geography. His interests include political and cultural relationships between Scotland and the United States and the manipulation of symbols and images by nationalist organisations. He has previously published on the Balkans, the Scottish National Party and Scottish football. Recently participating in a Staffordshire University project examining issues of leisure and exclusion, he edited a special issue of *North West Geographer* on this subject in 2000.

John Horne lectures in the sociology of sport and leisure at the University of Edinburgh. He is currently researching the social significance of the Korea/Japan 2002 World Cup, the concept of Japanization and sport in Japan. He is also preparing a book on *Sport in Consumer Culture*. His most recent publications include *Understanding Sport* (with Alan Tomlinson and Garry Whannel) Spon (1999), *Masculinities: Leisure Cultures, Identities and Consumption* (edited with Scott Fleming) Leisure Studies Publication No. 69 (2000) and 'Understanding Sport and Body Culture in Japan', in *Body & Society* Vol. 6, No. 2, pp. 73–86 (2000).

Lorna Jackson is a Senior Lecturer in the University of Edinburgh's Department of Physical Education, Sport and Leisure Studies. Her research interests are in nineteenth century social history of sport and leisure, and current research focuses on the influence of the 'aristocracy' (the county elite) on sport and popular pastimes in Argyllshire. Recent publications deal with the significance of Scottish Gaeldom in sport in Argyllshire, patronage of sport and popular leisure, and the role of the Volunteer movement in promoting sport.

Eleanor Lothian is Division Leader of Sport, Health and Leisure in the School of Social and Health Sciences at University of Abertay Dundee. Her MSc in Tourism, Scottish Hotel School was awarded by University of Strathclyde, Glasgow. Eleanor was formerly employed in the hotel industry in food development and leisure. Her research interests include tourism and development, tourism and politics, events and tourism.

Stephen Morrow is Senior Lecturer in the Department of Sports Studies at the University of Stirling. His academic background is in accountancy and finance and his research concentrates on financial aspects of the football industry. He has published papers on topics such as the accounting treatment of football players and thin trading in football club shares and is the author of The New Business of Football (Palgrave, 1999). Current research projects include 'Corporate Community Involvement in football clubs' and 'Ownership and governance in European Football Clubs' (a project funded by a FIFA sponsored scholarship).

Angela Phelps is a Principal Lecturer in the Department of International Studies, Nottingham Trent University, UK. Initially trained in biogeography, she continues to teach environmental issues within geography degrees. Angela is Subject Leader for Heritage Studies, managing modules in joint-honours schemes and post-graduate Heritage Management. Angela's research interests include the identification, management and interpretation of heritage landscapes and the management of visitors at heritage attractions. She has recent publications in Area and International Journal for Heritage Studies and has acted as a marketing consultant for The Galleries of Justice, Nottingham, Nottingham Transport Heritage Centre and the Design Museum, London.

Part One

Diffusion, Transformation
and Contestation

Anti-consumption or 'New' Consumption? Commodification, Identity and 'New Football'

Carlton Brick

**School of Sport, Exercise and Leisure,
University of Surrey Roehampton**

Introduction

English football has recently undergone a rapid and pronounced commodification[1]. The formation of the Carling sponsored Premier League in 1992 and the significant capital investment by subscription and satellite broadcasters have been identified as key moments in heralding the period that is generically referred to within the literature as the 'new football' or 'new commercialism' (Conn, 1999). There is also a general agreement within the literature that such developments have prompted transformations at the level of consumption and fandom, whereby the relationships that develop between the fan and the football club are now located within a globalised rather than localised market place.

There is now a significant body of literature devoted to the relations of consumption within football. Much of this literature begins with the premise that the commodification process works against fan interests in the game, and serves only to exclude the 'traditional fan' in favour of a 'new consumer' (Hamil *et al.*, 1999; Hamil *et al.*, 2000). In this paper I suggest that the literature tends to fetishise particularly forms of contemporary fandom as authentic and essential identities. Furthermore I suggest that these forms of fandom are themselves products of the current phase of commodification. Whilst formally resistant to the 'new consumption' of football they are compliant with and expressions of it themselves.

The methodology employed in this paper might be conceptualised as 'discursive anthropology.' Concerned with the discursive politics of authenticity within contemporary English football fandom, the research seeks to utilize Michel Foucault's (1998a, 1998b, 2000a, 2000b) theoretical framework of discourse. Foucault's emphasis

3

upon a genealogical approach to history, and the formulation of the power/knowledge nexus informs the analysis of two case studies concerning the fan cultures of leading English Premier League clubs, Manchester United and Newcastle United. Using interviews and participant observation of self-identified 'fan' groupings this research interrogates the relationships between the discursive formations of notions of 'fan' authenticity with the lived, concrete reality of supporting a football team.

Throughout the post-war period the patterns of football consumption have been patterns of flux and discontinuity. The 1950s were characterised by a marked fall in match attendance following the boom that accompanied the end of the previous decade. Walvin (1994) draws attention to the fact that whilst they fell dramatically during this period, attendance at football illustrated a shift away from the local club towards a polarisation around bigger and 'nationally' orientated clubs. The development of a relatively cheap and integrated transport network, the rise in television ownership and the increasing primacy of sport within television programme scheduling, combined (with other wider socio-political factors) to fracture the previously localised ways in which football was organised and consumed.

The processes of fracture has become more pronounced with the transformation of English football in the 1990s. The period has and continues to witness the development and expansion of football in multifarious and globally commodified forms. In its most immediate and obvious forms the rapid integration of digital and satellite broadcasting, and the potential developments at the level of internet broadcasting radically fracture, reinvent and recast the notion and act of spectating, and the privileged position of 'being there' within the cultural capital of fandom. The 1990s have been characterised in part, particularly at the level of elite Premier League football, by a culture of certification. Ownership, or access to a season ticket and other formalised relationships, such as club membership schemes, are necessary to 'gain access' to football. Such developments tend to mitigate against a more casual and informal mode of consumption, and become increasingly central to the construction of fan identities. The season ticket becomes commodified evidence of commitment and loyalty to the club.

Fandom has also been recast via state intervention, notably through the law. This is particularly true of the regulation of how the live spectacle should be watched and which 'styles' of fandom are and are not permitted. For example such juridical interventions as Lord Justice Taylor's enquiry and report into the 1989 Hillsborough disaster, the 1989 Football Supporters Act, and the 1991 Football (Offences) Act, (which has recently undergone two radical processes of amendment and now sites on the legislature as the Football (Disorder) Act), have resulted in a dramatic reconstruction of the 'match day experience', from sitting or standing, the consumption of alcohol, travelling to and from matches, and to the particular forms or 'styles' of behaviours, chants, language and other forms of expression that fans are permitted to engage in (see Brick, 2000 for a fuller assessment of these forms of legislative encroachment).

These developments provide context to a fuller analysis of current discourses on fandom, commodification and the market.

Member, customer and consumer

Chas Critcher (1979) adopts Raymond Williams (1961) historical model of cultural relationships between individuals (or social groups) and institutions — member, customer, and consumer — and applies them to football. Critcher (1979: p. 170) says of the relationships between individuals/social groups (football fans) and social institutions (football club):

> The first, however illusory, thinks of himself as a member, and may recognise an informal set of reciprocal duties and obligations between himself and the institution. The customer, more detached, is seeking satisfaction for specific wants: if they are not met over a certain period of time, he may somewhat reluctantly, take his patronage elsewhere. But the consumer has no loyalty or habit. He is informed of the choices open to him, and when he wants something will make rational choice about where he will get the best bargain.

This conceptualisation has been adopted as the dominant paradigm through which the development and transformations of contemporary English football are understood. Although I would add that whilst Critcher and Williams utilise these conceptualisations as a model of historical development, within much of the contemporary literature they are understood primarily as a typology. The member, the customer and the consumer being three distinct types of fandom which coexist, albeit rather fractiously, within the current game. The typology is shared by official, academic and popular accounts of the games commercial development. Economic marginalisation, social exclusion, and the cultural appropriation of the 'traditional' cultures of football fandom (the member) by an economic and cultural elite (the consumer) are dominant themes. The official rhetoric of English footballs contemporary administrative and regulatory bodies also reflect these distinctions:

> The commitment and loyalty of supporters to their football team is attractive in marketing terms. In the last ten years, ticket prices in the Football Association Premier League have risen by more than four times the rate of inflation (measured by the retail price index). Although rising prices are frequently ascribed to the need for stadium improvements, ticket price increases have been running at the same rate both before and after the Taylor Report. This suggests that prices have been increased largely to regulate demand. Football supporters are, by and large, committed enough to accept these increases, and demand is strong enough for those who are priced out of the market by others who are able to afford the cost of going to matches. (Smith and Le Juene, 1998: paragraph 2.8)

They continue:

> One matter of concern is the possibility that these new audiences may be less
> dedicated than existing core support. The new spectators have more cash and
> more choice. If they turn away from football as a result of the game's
> reputational problems, they may not be easy to replace. (Smith and Le Juene
> 1998: paragraph 2.9)

Similar conceptualisations have been made by academic responses to the
'consumerisation' of the football fan. Hamil (1999) draws upon the notion of 'fan
equity' (Salmon Brothers, 1997; Gorman and Calhoun, 1994) as the appropriate
conceptualisation of the fan, club, market relationship. Accordingly 'fan equity'
recognises the duality of the investment made by the football fan — emotional and
financial — which cut across typical interactions of the consumer/producer model
(Hamil, 1999: p. 29). Hamil (1999: p. 30) argues that the current phase of commercialisation within English football threatens to corrode the relationship of 'fan equity'.
Thus the processes of commodification are antithetical to 'fan equity' and are identified
as the key driving force behind the commercial trends dominant within the game. As
such Hamil suggests that there is a 'traditional fan' located outside the contemporary
cultures of commercialisation and commodification currently appropriating the game.
King (1998: p. 141) on the other hand suggests:

> The consumption of football differs significantly from this conventional model
> of [consumption], for the fan does not simply purchase what the club presents
> to the fans. The commodity which the fans buy is not confined to the players
> whom they watch; the fans also purchase the atmosphere which they
> themselves create in watching the match.

Both King and Hamil consider the fan a distinct and unique consumer, yet locate the
fan within their respective models quite differently. According to Hamil the fan is
external and located outside the commodification process. King on the other hand
considers the fan as a consumer located very much within the current commodification
process. The conception of fandom as an active and integral agent within the cultures
of commodification and commercialisation, rather than passive and external is an
important one. Firstly it offers an analytical framework which resists the tendency
towards essentialist and a priori constructions of contemporary fandom as either 'traditional' or 'new consumers'. Secondly it resits the tendency towards the counterposition
of the commodification process as a purely destructive and negative process that
characterises much of the academic literature on football.

The fetish of 'being there'

Much of this literature tends towards a fetishisation of particular ways of consuming
football. Privilege is often accorded to the live match going spectator as the only

authentic form of consuming. Cannon and Hamil (2000) employ this fetishised conceptualisation as a methodological and analytic tool to classify different typologies of fandom as consumers. They draw definite and particular distinctions between on the one-hand fans and on the other, supporters. They argue that:

> The line between fans and supporters is important as it distinguishes between fans who have positive attitudes to a team but do not, usually, have any active involvement e.g. through attending games; and supporters who have an active involvement e.g. through attending games. (Cannon and Hamil, 2000: p. 37)

The implication is that to be an authentic follower of the game one can only consume football by 'being there'. As such they go on to suggest that the exclusion and marginalisation of this authentic supporter has occurred apace through the conscious marketing of the game towards the inauthentic fan:

> In Manchester United's case, for example, there are around three million fans but fewer than 150, 000 supporters. Some planned developments, notably pay TV, seem likely to further discriminate in favour of fans against supporters. (Cannon and Hamil, 2000: p. 37)

The significance of the separation between fan and supporter is two fold. Such a conceptualisation of the commodification process as a means by which fixed and essentialist notions of fandom(s) are excluded or included masks the fluidity and multifarious ways within which fans interact and (re) connect with the contemporary game. Secondly the readiness to accept these constructions of fandom as an a priori given blinds investigation to fandom's active engagement with and utilisation of the commodification process in the increment of cultural capital, and the contestation of cultural spaces. I will endeavour to explore this further by firstly attempting to illustrate how sections of contemporary fandom relocate and redefine the experience of 'being there', and secondly through a discussion of the development of during the 1990s of what the literature refers to as fan power or fan empowerment (Giulianotti, 1997; Williams, 1992).

Relocating the 'live'

With the advent of satellite and subscription television football as a 'live' experience has undergone a marked redefinition. Whilst Cannon and Hamil (2000) claim that these developments are actively excluding supporters in favour of more distant and passive fans, I would suggest that the process is not so clear cut and is in fact far more ambiguous than suggested. Whilst it may be the case that supporters are actively excluded from the 'live' experience by increased price rises, or through footballs courting of the 'new consumer', it is also the case that often that so called excluded supporters will reintegrate, reconstruct and redefine the cultures surrounding the game by utilising the very processes and technological developments that are assumed to have marginalised them in the first place. Significantly it is often the fan themselves who seek to consciously exclude themselves from the stadium as a site of 'live' consumption.

Nash (2000: p. 58) reports of Liverpool season ticket holders giving up their tickets before kick of on a match day and choosing to watch the game in what they perceive as a "communal and participatory fashion" within the relative freedom of the pub atmosphere. Armstrong's substantive study of core groups of Sheffield United supporters suggests similar trends. Armstrong reports of groups of supporters consciously rejecting to attend games because of price rises and the increasingly authoritarian regulation and surveillance the modern fan is subjected to. As such, "At times, 150 would gather in pubs, minutes from Bramall Lane, only to watch their team on satellite TV" (Armstrong, 1998: p. 332). Indeed it is perhaps worth floating the question as to whether it is possible to be excluded from or marginalised from the cultures of the game when these cultures are so obviously redefined and expanded as new modes of consumption bypass and subverts traditionally privileged forms of consumption.

For some fans, both season ticket holders and regular attendees, 'being there' is considered, at times, a lesser experience than consuming football in other ways[2]. A notable phenomenon has been the emergence of what could be described as a 'topophobic' relationship with the 'home' game[3]. These fans quite frequently seek to relocate and recreate the fan carnivalesque in an environment they consider more amicable and sympathetic to their style of fandom. The Public House often becomes the site for such a relocation, which they contrasted quite explicitly with the impersonal, sanitised and sterile environment of the modern football stadium. These fans indicated that the biggest problem with watching live football has been the reconfiguration of football grounds. The advent of restricted ticketing and seating has for these fans resulted in communal groupings having been broken up and dispersed. These developments dramatically transform what might be considered as the match day experience. Particularly notable is the significance acquired by pre and post match drinking as a focus for communal and shared experience on match day. Consciously abstaining from what they consider to be the increasingly inauthentic, fragmentary, and intrusive manufacture of the match going experience, for sections of fandom 'being there' is no-longer an essential experience but has become the antithesis of what they consider going to watch football is all about.

Fandom as commodified contestation

During the late 1980s and 1990s a 'fan voice' has emerged within the games sociopolitical cultures. Fan orientated radio talk shows and phone-ins and other interactive media such as the Internet have fed into a process whereby a fan discourse has established itself as a discrete cultural space. A dominant presence within this cultural space has been the expansion of organised fandom in the form of the independent fanzine and the independent fan organisation.

By the late 1980s the apparent decline in reported cases of hooliganism and the emergence of new fan representative groups, such as the national FSA (Football Supporters Association) and club specific ISAs (Independent Supporters Associations) indicate a marked transformation in footballs consumption. The emergence in the late 1980s of the FSA and other fan representative groups marks a break with previous forms and styles of fan organisation. Formed in 1927 the NATFED (National Federation of Football Supporters Clubs) was until the late 1980s the only co-ordinated representative body within fandom. Largely reflective of a passive, officially sanctioned form of localised consumption the NATFED was effectively surpassed as the voice of fandom with the shifts that occurred in the late 1980s towards more active and agitational styles of consumption. Fandom emerges out of the 1980s, apparently empowered by the discourse of consumer rights, conceptually and structurally different from the types of fandom that preceeded[4]. Above all the new fandom represented a dramatically new consumption of football. This brings to the fore a number of important tensions and paradoxes. Non more so that whilst being perceived as one of the most vociferous and consistent critics of the 'new consumption' of football, the rise of independent forms of fandom in the late 1980s are an integral part of the 'new consumption' itself.

Within much of the sociological and academic literature these new forms of organised fandom are presented as forms of resistance to the commodification of football. According to King (1998: p. 190) IMUSA (Independent Manchester United Supporters Association) and its subculture are representative of an active process whereby it is "developing strategies of resistance against the new consumption of football". But rather than resisting, organised fan groups and representative bodies (such as ISAs and fanzines) are actively engaging in the 'new consumption'. The process is not one of resistance but cultural contestation. Such a distinction is important as it resists the tendency within much of the literature to adopt the position that the processes of commodification and commercialisation are unilaterally negative. They are quite simply not. But nor are they simply positive. Rather these processes are utilised by 'fan voices' that contest the cultural and discursive spaces within contemporary football, which have been created by the commodification and commercialisation processes themselves.

Furthermore King (1998: p. 190-191) suggests that the 'notion of authenticity' generated within such subcultures "undermines the flat one-dimensionality of the notion of the consumer". Whilst this may be the case, subcultural symbols and notions of fan authenticity are very much produced and circulated within the process of commodification and commercialisation dominant in the game. Fanzines are an example of fandom taking a new commodified form. They are also key definers and producers of notions of authenticity.

Commodification and the carnivalesque

Of late concern has been expressed regarding a crisis of atmosphere within many of the country's largest and most well attended ground. The literature often points to the removal of a 'traditional' fan base and their replacement with a family orientated, consumer audience as a source of this crisis (see Brick (2000) for a discussion of the limits of these critiques). Sir Alex Ferguson, the manager of Manchester United, has voiced similar concerns (Brick, 1997; The Sun 15 March 2000: p. 41). As a result the official administrative and regulatory bodies within football have felt compelled to respond.

In April 1997 the FA Premier League commissioned a report on crowd atmosphere (Carling *et al.*, 1997). The report tentatively suggests the widespread establishment of 'atmosphere areas'. Over a number of years now spectators have been subjected to club schemes to manufacture atmosphere. Cheer leaders, loud music played over the tannoy when teams take to the field, score goals at half time etc. There have been numerous complaints within the Manchester United fanzines against the intrusion of the tannoy when playing loud music to mark a United victory. A number of clubs have given official sanction for the formation of fan musical bands to orchestrate and lead fan chants[5]. At Arsenal an officially sanctioned song sheet was produced and handed out to fans prior to the 1999 F.A Cup semi- final against Manchester United[6]. These official attempts to manufacture atmosphere are a means of disciplining and limiting the scope and content of the spontaneous fan carnivalesque. King (1998: p. 141) argues that:

> The consumption of football differs significantly from this conventional model [of consumption], for the football fan does not simply purchase what the club presents to the fans. The commodity which fans buy is not confined to the players whom they watch; the fans also purchase the atmosphere which they themselves create in watching the match.

King points to the centrality of the fan within the creation and cultivation of atmosphere. Furthermore King locates the fan within the process of commodification. The fans active role in the creation of atmosphere and the carnivalesque is a key part of the product the fan pays to consume. This insight stands in contradistinction to Kings claim, noted above, that fan organisations such as IMUSA are instrumental in a process whereby strategies are developed to resist the 'new consumption' of football. Rather, it seems, it is the very centrality of the fan within the production of the commodity they consume that has lead to a further commodification and institutionalisation of contemporary fandom. Furthermore independent fan organisations seem compliant with this process. The idea of 'atmosphere areas' or 'singing sections' has received fairly unanimous support from the independent supporters associations, and they have become one of the most consistent supporters of the idea. Indeed such a demand has been a founding principle of IMUSA since their formation in 1995. Such has been the demand that Manchester United have at the start of the 2000/01 season set a side a section of their Old Trafford ground, called the 'Fan Zone', to encourage a more spontaneous and traditional style of support. Whilst the notion of an atmosphere area may seem appealing as a means of cultivating what might be termed a traditional style of support, such schemes function primarily as means of disciplining and controlling the very forms of support and carnivalesque they are designed to encourage.

Furthermore the Old Trafford 'Fan Zone' implies that everybody else in the rest of the ground are not officially sanctioned fans and as such I presume inauthentic. In this respect access to the 'Fan Zone' becomes symbolic of a privileged and authentic commodified fandom, i.e.: you buy a ticket to this specially sanctioned area. As an officially sanctioned 'zone' which facilitates a certain ascribed type or style of fandom, does this then mean that those not 'in the zone' so to speak, who either attempt to participate in or create their own carnivalseque are subject to a form of official censor? Indeed it is not only those outside the zone who are subject to this ascribed form of control, but those within as they become subject to ascribed codes of conduct as a means of gaining access in the first place (Brick, 2000: p. 162).

The establishment of 'singing sections' or 'Fan Zones' is consistent with and compliant in the commodification and control of fandom, whereby fans purchase special access to designated parts of the ground which have been ascribed as officially controlled and surveyed areas of fan activity.

Conclusion

In this paper I have argued that the forms of fandom that have emerged as responses to the current phases of English footballs commercialisation, engage with rather than resist the commodification process. The forms of contemporary fandom are themselves a part of the 'new consumption' which they so often predicate themselves against. It has not been my intention to illustrate to posit an alternative, true and resistant fandom. To suggest as much would be consistent with the theoretical and analytical positions I have attempted to critique in this paper. Rather it has been my intention to posit that contemporary fandom is not distinct but compliant with the commodification process. I have illustrated that academic accounts critical of the commodification of football tend towards a false oppositionalism between the market and fandom (particularly in its organisational forms). The interactions between fandom and the commodification process are much more ambiguous and fluid than the simplistic models of resistance and appropriation imply. Indeed, fandom, by its own volition, is a product of the very process it is claimed it is resisting. Rather than resisting, fandom actively contests and subverts aspects of the commodification process. It does this in a number of different ways, which have a number of different outcomes, some of which I have outlined above. The emergence of critical fan discourses, notably the fanzines and fan representative groups, are not distinct and external, but very much a part and parcel of the 'new consumption' of football.

Such oppositionalism is not confined to the literature critiqued in this paper. It is a significant feature of the literature that seeks to distance itself from the current preoccupation of the 'new consumer' versus 'traditional fan' dichotomy. Sociologist Ian Taylor has argued:

> If, with the editors of fanzines and the organisers of the Football Supporters Association, we spend too much time bemoaning the loss of the 'true' terrace football follower, we may be missing the significance of the emergence, rather closer to home, of new ways of being a fan, for example, and new ways of proclaiming, in an increasingly globalised world, one's local origin and identity. (Taylor, cited in Williams 2000: p. 103)

To do as Taylor suggests, to reject the "bemoaning" of the loss of the authentic fan, would only serve to skew and mystify the very project he demands. The "bemoaning", as he calls it, of an imagined football culture, and the discourses of crisis and loss that permeate both academic and popular accounts of the current transformation of English football are an intrinsic and explicit expressions of the 'new consumption' and the "new ways" in which fan identities are constructed, conceptualised and expressed. They are as important as the advent and impact of the global media, or the fact that Manchester United has an apparently thriving fan base in East Asia.

Finally, returning to Critcher's model — member, customer and consumer — that rather than being distinct and exclusive fan types as suggested by much of the literature, I would argue that they are simultaneous expressions of both desired and actual relationships between the fan and the football club that occur within contemporary fandom in all its multifarious forms.

Notes

1   Abercrombie (1996: p. 110) defines commodification thus, "as the process by which more and more goods, services or human relationships become tradeable in a market and produced for profit." This is the general meaning used in this paper.

2   The observations and themes made in this section are based upon research amongst predominantly male, white football fans of Manchester United and Newcastle United, most of who are aged between 30 and 40 years. Although these self-selecting groupings of fans were not always exclusively male and white, the congregation of these fans within pubs is itself exclusionary against other fans. These forms of exclusion were not rationalised directly in terms of ethnicity or gender but in terms of authenticity and style i.e. the types of carnivalesque these fans sought to define themselves against. Significantly the theme of safety, or feeling safe would crop up in these fans articulations of why they would prefer to watch football in such an environment. For this group of predominantly white, male and older fans the public house provided a 'safer'

environment as it afforded a certain degree of control and freedom regarding the production of their carnivalesque. This was contrasted with the 'unsafe' environment of the football stadium. An environment they perceived as heavily regulated and individuating. Conversely, other fans in my research would counterpose the safety of watching football in the stadium to the 'unsafe' environment of a public house. James, a 22 year old, black Manchester United fan from London said, "I don't like watching football in pubs. I mean it depends on the game I suppose, but when you're in a pub you've got all different types of people depending on what type of pub it is ... I can only see there being trouble so that's why I wouldn't go" (Personal interview, 4 July 2000).

3   A consistent theme that emerges through my research interviews with fans who regularly follow their clubs home and away is their regard of away fixtures as a more 'pleasurable' or 'authentic' experience. This is usually rationalised in terms of the relative 'freedom' now accorded to away fans. Together within one section of the ground, and usually afforded more 'liberty' than home fans by the policing authorities, the carnivalesque of the away fan takes on a greater significance as it is contrasted with what is perceived as the highly regulated culture of surveillance encountered when watching "our team, in our own ground" (Mike, 35 year old, Manchester United 'regular'. Personal interview 5 March 1999).

4   One should also include the development of shareholder fan organisations such as SU (Shareholder United) at Manchester United which emerged out of the fan opposition to Rupert Murdoch's attempted take-over of Manchester United. The Government has since launched the Supporters Direct initiative to encourage the establishment of shareholding fan groups.

5   Ironically one such officially sanctioned band at Sheffield Wednesday have been banned from a number of grounds because of complaints regarding the intrusive and manufactured nature of their carnivalesque.

6   The song sheets, which also double up as yellow display cards (Arsenals away strip), include such instructions to fans as "If you're wearing yellow, make sure it's visible and not hidden behind a coat or jumper", and "Use your card again for spontaneous repeat showings and Mexican Waves throughout the game". The songs fans are 'asked' to sing include the rather difficult "We've got Dennis Bergkamp" a song that comprises of simply repeating said sentence over and over again, and the paean to Arsenals Nigerian striker, Kanu which simply requires the repetition of the player's name over and over again, although the song sheet does stress that one elongate the players name to achieve maximum effect, thus "Kann-ooh, Kann-ooh, Kann-ooh."

References

Abercrombie, N. (1996) 'Cultural values and commodification: the case of the publishing industry', in A. Godley and O. Westall (eds) *Business history and business culture.* Manchester: Manchester University Press.

Armstrong, G. (1998) Football hooligans: Knowing the score. Oxford: Berg.

Brick, C. (2000) 'Taking offence: Modern moralities and the perception of the football fan', in J. Garland, D. Malcolm and M. Rowe (eds) *The future of football: Challenges for the twenty-first century*. London: Frank Cass, pp. 158–172.

Brick, C. (1997) 'We're not singing anymore', *90 Minutes* 26 April 1997: pp. 30–31.

Cannon, T. and Hamil, S. (2000) 'Reforming football's boardrooms', in S. Hamil, J. Michie, C. Oughton and S. Warby (eds) *Football in the digital age: Whose game is it anyway?*. Edinburgh: Mainstream, pp. 36–46.

Carling, P. Highmore, S. Sillitoe, S. and Johns, P. (1997) *Crowd atmosphere at Premier League matches*. London: FA Premier League.

Critcher, C. (1979) 'Football since the War', in J. Clarke, C. Critcher and R. Johnson (eds) *Working class culture: Studies in history and theory*. London: Hutchinson, pp. 161–184.

Conn, D. (1999) 'The new commercialism', in S. Hamil, J. Michie, C. Oughton, C. (eds) *A game of two halves: The business of football*. Edinburgh: Mainstream, pp: 40–55.

Foucault, M. (1998a) 'Nietzsche, genealogy, history', in J. D. Faubion (ed) *Michel Foucault. Aesthetics, method, and epistemology. Essential works of Foucault 1954-1984*, volume two. Harmondsworth: Penguin Books, pp: 369–391.

——— (1998b) 'On the archaeology of the sciences. Response to the Epistemology Circle', in J. D. Faubion, (ed) *Michel Foucault. Aesthetics, method, and epistemology. Essential works of Focault 1954-1984* volume two, Harmondsworth: Penguin Books, pp. 297–333.

——— (2000a) 'The subject and power', in Faubion, J. D. (ed) *Michel Foucault. Power. Essential works of Foucault 1954-1984* volume three. Harmondsworth: The Penguin Press, pp. 326–348.

——— (2000b) *The archaeology of knowledge*. London: Routledge.

Gorman, J. and Calhoun, K. (1994) *The name of the game: The business of sports*. New York: John Wiley and Sons.

Giulianotti, R. (1997) 'Enlightening the North. Aberdeen fanzines and local football identity', in G. Armstrong and R. Giulianotti (eds) *Entering the field, new perspectives on world football*. Oxford: Berg, pp: 211-237.

Hamil, S. Michie, J. and Oughton, C. (1999) (eds) *A game of two halves: The business of football*. Edinburgh: Mainstream.

Hamil, S. Michie, J. Oughton, C. and Warby, S. (eds) (2000) *Football in the digital age: whose game is it anyway?*. Edinburgh: Mainstream.

King, A. (1998) *The end of the terraces: The transformation of English football in the 1990s*. London: Leicester University Press.

Nash, R. (2000) 'The sociology of English football in the 1990s: fandom, business and future research', *Football Studies* Vol. 3, No. 1: pp. 49–62.

Salmon Brothers (1997) 'UK football clubs: valuable assets?', *Global equity research: leisure*. London: Salmon Brothers.

Smith, Sir J. and Le Jeune, M. (1998) *Football: Its values, finances and reputation*. London: The Football Association.

Walvin, J. (1994) *The people's game: The history of football revisited*. Edinburgh: Mainstream.

Williams, R. (1961) *The long revolution*. Harmondsworth: Penguin.

Williams, J. (1992) 'Thugs and kisses', in *When Saturday Comes* No: 59 (January).

——— (2000) 'The changing face of football: a case for national regulation?', in S. Hamil, J. Michie, C. Oughton and S. Warby (eds) *Football in the digital age: whose game is it anyway?*. Edinburgh: Mainstream, pp. 94–106.

Football Clubs on the Stock Exchange: An Inappropriate Match? The Case of Celtic plc

Stephen Morrow

Department of Sports Studies, University of Stirling

Following the approach by BT Wolfensohn, the financial advisers to a consortium which includes the venture capitalists BT Capital Partners Europe, Kenny Dalglish, Jim Kerr and others (together, the 'Consortium'), the Board of Celtic plc has, after careful consideration with its advisers Greig Middleton & Co. Limited and Nomura International plc, concluded that the Consortium's proposals are not in the best interests of the ordinary and preference shareholders of Celtic.

The Board remains of the view that it is in the best long-term interests of Celtic for Mr McCann's shareholding to be offered to existing shareholders and season-book holders of Celtic and to other individual investors who are keenly interested in the long-term success of Celtic.

(Announcement to the London Stock Exchange by the Board of Celtic plc, 18 December 1998)

Introduction

As has been well documented, the 1990s has seen football plc welcomed onto the Stock Exchange. As of May 1999 there are 21 clubs listed on the London market: 14 on the Official List and seven on the Alternative Investment Market (AIM). To date the amount raised by clubs which have floated totals £167m. At 30 June 1998 market capitalisation for listed clubs was £1,063m, down from a peak of £1,899m (Deloitte & Touche, 1998). Market listing for clubs is also becoming more usual in other European countries. Clubs are now listed in Denmark, Italy and Holland. It is also expected that German clubs such as Bayern Munich and Borussia Dortmund will shortly seek market listings.

However, it is often asserted that football is more than just a business. In this paper the stakeholder concept is utilised to provide a fuller understanding of the nature of contemporary football clubs. The paper addresses issues of ownership within football clubs, focusing not only on providers of capital as owners but also on other stakeholder groups who, it is argued, have proprietary claims. Notwithstanding the recent trend of clubs having their shares listed on the Stock Exchange, the paper continues by questioning the extent to which Stock Exchange listed companies are the appropriate vehicles for contemporary football clubs. In particular it focuses on the case of Celtic plc. Implications arising out of its market listing and proposed changes in the ownership of Celtic plc are used to consider the case for alternative forms of organisational structure for Celtic in particular, and for football clubs more generally.

The stakeholder concept

In studies into the objectives of football clubs carried out in the 1970s and 1980s it was fairly common to describe clubs as utility maximisers, seeking to maximise playing success while remaining solvent (Sloane 1971, 1980; Sutherland and Haworth, 1986; Arnold and Benveniste, 1987). However, it has been argued that football's rush to the capital market place has brought with it a more shareholder-centric focus and a greater emphasis on the generation of profit and the maximisation of shareholder value (Conn, 1997: p. 154, Lee, 1999: p. 86). The floating of football clubs on the Stock Exchange has led to less concentrated ownership structures at many clubs (Morrow, 1999, pp. 78–83). This in turn has led to improved governance as directors have been obliged to recognise the rights of other shareholders (Morrow, 1999: p. 87). Interestingly, however, as football has focused more on maximisation of shareholder value and the concomitant accountability to shareholders, much of the focus in wider political and business communities has been on alternative and more inclusive models of corporate behaviour and governance.

The most commonly discussed alternative model of *Corporate Governance* and behaviour is the stakeholder model. A stakeholder can be defined as "any group or individual who can affect or is affected by the achievement of the firm's objectives" (Freeman, 1984). While most commentators would argue that a company's stakeholders would typically include its management, employees, customers, suppliers, owners, competitors and the community (however defined), critics argue that the definition is so wide that it includes practically everyone, everything, everywhere (Sternberg, 1998: p. 94). Two key aspects of stakeholder theory are, first, that corporations are accountable to all their stakeholders, and second, that a major objective of management is to balance the conflicting demands of the various stakeholders in the corporation (Ansoff, 1987: p. 51).

The stakeholder model was integral to the 1995 inquiry by the Royal Society for the Encouragement of Arts, Commerce and Manufactures into Tomorrow's Company (RSA, 1995). It concluded that financial success for tomorrow's company is dependent on the adoption of an inclusive approach to business, one which focuses on all stakeholder relationships, not just those with shareholders. This is akin to the notion of a stakeholder economy espoused by Tony Blair. Drawing on the ideas of such as Will Hutton (Hutton, 1995) and John Kay (Kay, 1993), the Blair vision is of an inclusive society and economy in which all social groups have a stake in the wellbeing of corporations and the national economy.

Football's stakeholders

It can be argued that the stakeholder concept has greater relevance for football clubs than for more conventional business organisations because of the particular features of certain football club stakeholders, specifically their demands for accountability. Consideration is required in particular of a club's direct or traditional community, namely its supporters, and of a wider notion of community encompassing people and groups affected by the existence of a football club within their environment. While this broader community is most commonly defined in terms of geography, it might also include religious or social dimensions.

Supporters as stakeholders

The importance of supporters in this stakeholder model of football clubs has been recognised by several authors (Conn, 1997; King, 1997; Lee, 1999; Morrow, 1999). The traditional notion of a club's supporters has been to view them as the club's community. Perhaps the best analogy is with a church. A church is more than a physical building: it is a community of people who come together to worship, i.e. the worshippers become the church. Traditionally the relationship between a football team, the stadium and the supporters has been something similar: together they become the club.

As mentioned earlier it has been argued that the incorporation of football has been accompanied by a more shareholder-centric focus, with a greater emphasis being placed on the generation of profit and the maximisation of shareholder value. Along with these changes, it has become frequent to refer to supporters as customers. This notion of supporters as customers reduces football to free market economics: people will pay more for better services. The logic of the customer applies equally to ticket pricing, the price of merchandising or whatever. Taken to its rational conclusion the supporter as a customer even has the choice of which team to support. The customer gets what he pays for: the rights of supporters are restricted to the economic rights of non-purchase.

Supporters are obviously important to clubs in economic terms whether through purchasing season tickets, merchandising or whatever. However, there are strong arguments which suggest that the 'customer' description of the relationship between supporters and clubs is not adequate. In economic terms it is incomplete because it fails to consider the role played by the supporters in creating the product that they are asked to buy — i.e. football supporters are asked to buy what they themselves are helping to create, the spectacle of support (King, 1997). More importantly, in social and political terms, the concept of the customer fails to capture the idea of a supporter's identity with a club. The sense of attachment between a supporter and his or her club is usually very strong. In addition, the relationship is usually a long-term relationship, although there is some evidence to suggest that changing club attachments may be increasing in the new generation of fans in the FA Premier League (SNCCFR, 1997). Nevertheless for most supporters supporting a football club is like membership of a particular church or faith — conversion is possible but happens fairly infrequently (Morrow, 1999: p. 168).

Stakeholder theory holds that the strategies adopted by managers should enable them to manage those stakeholder relationships which are most crucial to the corporation's success (Roberts, 1998). Accordingly the management of this key relationship with supporters should be seen as crucial to the success of the football company.

The community as a stakeholder

In the UK professional sporting organisations have a deep-rooted identification with a particular city or region and hence community. The importance of clubs can be both economic and sentimental. Clubs can act as focal points for communities, something to rally around and bring people together, whether at times of success such as a Cup run, or at times of difficulty such as when a club is threatened by financial problems. Football clubs can also be a way of promoting a town or area. Even normally impassive banks are susceptible to the notion of football clubs as community resources, with evidence to suggest that lending decisions made by banks are not always made on commercial grounds (Morrow, 1997a).

The RSA Inquiry's vision of Tomorrow's Company (RSA, 1995) recognised the importance of a company's community:

> Tomorrow's company recognises its interdependence with the community in which it operates. It develops leadership strategies which strengthen both the climate for business success and the community itself.

The importance of community was also recognised in a football context in the report commissioned by the Football Association on 'Football — its Values, Finances and Reputation' (Smith, 1997). The report included a draft Code of Conduct for football clubs which identified two challenges in terms of a club's community: firstly, to demonstrate that it is a vital part of its community, and secondly, to remember that community role when making decisions.

On an ongoing basis, however, many clubs are remote from anything other than their direct community of supporters. Rather than the club being a source of leisure or recreational facilities within a community, many local residents are likely to view a football club as something which brings inconvenience to their normal life at every home match. This could range from traffic chaos through to uncivilised individual and group behaviour (and possibly also hooliganism) being brought closer to them than they would wish. Given the deep-rooted identification that exists between football clubs and their communities more could be done by clubs to adopt an inclusive approach to those communities. Many suggestions have been put forward as to how clubs can overcome their remoteness from the wider community, ranging from the use of training facilities as sports centres through to using the grounds for things like Mother and Toddler classes (Morrow, 1999: p. 193; Perryman, 1998). One model for football is the way in which churches have found an important role to play in communities, seven days a week. This is particularly significant given that most churches, unlike football clubs at present, have to deal with a dwindling direct community in terms of falling congregations.

A critique of the stakeholder model

The stakeholder concept is appealing as it captures more fully the nature of football clubs and the groups who can affect or are affected by the achievement of the club's objectives. But the concept is not without its problems, chief of which centres on actually defining the objectives of football clubs. However, it is argued that this problem is also relevant in the wider corporate environment. Sternberg (1998) suggests that according to stakeholder theory there is only one legitimate organisational objective: balanced stakeholder benefits. However, this objective is accompanied by three problems: first, a lack of guidance as to how stakeholder groups should be selected, second, a failure to explain what should count as a benefit for the purposes of balancing benefits, and third, a lack of guidance on how the balance should be struck.

It has been argued that, prior to becoming Stock Exchange listed companies, football clubs could be assumed to have a unitary objective — playing success subject to a solvency constraint. For example, McMaster (1997) argues that everyone at a club from the board of directors to the players and coaching staff is interested in maximising their utility, a factor dependent to some extent on relative playing success. This view was not universally shared. In a paper on the operation of the retain and transfer system, Stewart (1986) argued that the existence of this system, which operated to restrict players' labour market mobility, was recognition of the fact that without it players would operate in a manner consistent with the pursuit of their own rather than their employers' objectives. Post-Bosman[1] players are now much freer to operate in a manner consistent with their own objectives rather than their employers' objectives. This, however, is no different from the situation that other organisations find themselves in.

In the new business of football the objective of supporters remains the attainment of football success. Contemporary football clubs, in particular those clubs which are listed on the Stock Exchange, face particular problems where other stakeholders have different, and often conflicting objectives. For example, where the club's shareholders are not drawn exclusively from the club's supporters, then the investment motives of at least some of these shareholders will be in terms of earning a financial return. As the following quote illustrates, whether the discussion is in terms of balancing the benefits to stakeholders or balancing the objectives of stakeholders, for Stock Exchange listed companies such as Manchester United, conflict is almost inevitable:

> As for the suggestion from City analysts that [Manchester] United should give its extra money [a cash surplus of £39m reported in its 1997 accounts] back to shareholders, Mitten's response [Andy Mitten, editor of United We Stand, a Manchester United supporters' fanzine] highlights the shareholder-supporter divide that runs through all stock market-quoted clubs.
>
> He says: "These profits have come out of the fans' pockets, in the form of gate receipts, merchandising and television revenue, yet they end up going to some anonymous, faceless investor in the City? That's not right." ('City eyes United's cash hoard', *The Financial Times* 21 November 1997: p. 12)

For Stock Exchange listed clubs such as Manchester United, the adoption of an inclusive or stakeholding approach may seem like little more than an idle dream. Nevertheless, various suggestions have been put forward to try to deal with this conflict and to encourage a more inclusive approach to business, such as the creation of some sort of regulatory structure which would protect the rights of supporter-stakeholders (Football Task Force, 1999; Hamil, 1999; Perryman, 1998). Perhaps of greater significance is the decision taken in April 1999 by the Secretary of State for Trade and Industry, Stephen Byers, to follow the advice of the Monopolies and Mergers Commission and reject BSkyB's bid for Manchester United (a bid supported by the directors but rejected by many stakeholder groups)[2], a decision which may prove to be a watershed for governance of football in the UK.

In this paper, however, the focus is on alternative types of ownership structure which may more fully capture the nature of a football club and its stakeholders. These alternative ownership structures are of relevance given that the philosophical antecedents of stakeholder theory reach back to the 19th Century, to the conceptions of the co-operative movement and mutuality (Clarke, 1998). These alternative ownership structures will be discussed after a consideration of the case of Celtic plc.

The case of Celtic plc: a model for change?

In this section governance, accountability and the ownership framework of contemporary football clubs will be considered using the example of Celtic plc. Celtic is a good example for many reasons: it is listed on the main market of the Stock Exchange, it is one of the largest British clubs in terms of market capitalisation, it has strong links with its community, it has a high number of supporter shareholders and most importantly of all it is undergoing changes to its ownership structure, with plans by the club's chairman to dispose of his majority holding in the club to supporters and season-book holders.

The official centenary history of Celtic, written by the Labour MP Brian Wilson, begins by noting that the club was established for reasons closely related to Irish identity and Catholic charity (Wilson, 1988: p. 1). Founded in 1888 by a Marist Brother, Brother Walfrid, the club's principal objective was to raise money to provide food for the poor in the East End of Glasgow. From these charitable origins Celtic went on to become the first British club to win the European Cup in 1967. To this day the club continues to have its roots deep in the Glasgow Irish community from whose descendants it still draws much of its support.

While conscious of the club's history and the importance to its community, the club's current directors have worked hard to present Celtic as a non-sectarian, Scottish institution. This is clear from the club's Social Mission statement which states that:

> Celtic Football Club is a Scottish football club with proud Irish links. The primary business of Celtic is as a football club. It is run on a professional basis with no political agenda. However, the Club has a wider role and the responsibility of being a major Scottish social institution promoting health, well-being and social integration.

The club's charitable objectives and acknowledgement of its community role are explicitly referred to in its annual report:

> Celtic Football Club is committed to supporting the community and is proud today that it strives to honour the charitable objectives of the Club's founders. (Celtic plc Annual Report year ended 30 June 1998)[3]

It is interesting to contrast the history of Celtic with that of another famous European football club, the Spanish club Barcelona. While Celtic was formed at least in part to help preserve the identity of the incoming Irish in Glasgow, by contrast Barcelona, although founded by foreigners (mostly British and Swiss residents), quickly assumed the main objectives of Catalan society (L'Elefant Blau, 1999). Nevertheless despite the different community focus of the two clubs, what is clear is that since their foundation over 100 years ago both clubs have continued to play an important role within their communities, a point that will be returned to later in this paper.

Fergus McCann became the owner of Celtic in March 1994, taking over a club which was beset with internal disputes and shareholder and supporter unrest and had been within eight minutes of being put into liquidation. He provided an immediate cash guarantee to stabilise the company's borrowings, following this up with a rights issue and other subscriptions which raised in aggregate over £12m for the company, eliminating bank and other major debts.

Part of McCann's strategy for turning around the ailing club was to make a public share issue. The issue took place in January 1995 and remains one of the most success-ful share issues ever made by a football club, raising £9.4m for the Club and creating 10,500 new shareholders. Despite January being generally recognised as a bad month for raising capital the issue was oversubscribed some 1.8 times. The minimum sub-scription was £620 per unit, each unit representing five ordinary and five preference shares, with the issue price of the ordinary shares being £64 per share. Since flotation the share price peaked at £525 per share on 6 January 1997. In September 1998 the club carried out a 100 for one share split. As at 8 April 1999 the shares were trading at £3.50 per share.

Since McCann's takeover Celtic has gone from strength to strength, both on and off the field. The club won its first Premier Division title in ten years in season 1997/98, while in season 1998/99 the team played in front of highest number of season ticket holders of any British club (52,543), making it the fifth best supported team in the world after Barcelona, Real Madrid, Inter Milan and Borussia Dortmund. These supporters are all seated in the largest modern football stadium in Britain (capacity 60,400), a project completed with no mortgage or government funding. Financially the club has reported substantial increases in turnover and profits over the last five years (see Table 1).

Table 1: Five year record (years ended 30 June)

	1994 £000	1995 £000	1996 £000	1997 £000	1998 £000
Turnover	8,736	10,376	16,005	22,189	27,821
Profit from operations	282	669	2,735	5,899	5,094
(Loss)/Profit after tax	(1,404)	(401)	(1,013)	5,152	7,10
Stadium investment to date	8,694	23,335	34,690	37,011	46,764

Source: Celtic plc Annual Report year ended 30 June 1998

One distinctive factor about the Celtic share issue was that the shares were bought almost exclusively by supporters of the club, as opposed to city institutions. No formal research has been carried out into the reasons for the high take-up of shares by supporters. However, one reason put forward is access supporters had to loans from the Co-operative Bank, which it is argued helped ensure that it was investors who were looking to the long term who were successful in acquiring shares, rather than those seeking to make a quick profit (Morrow, 1997b). Other factors, related to the nature of the club's history and community, can also be put forward as possible explanations.

One driving force in the emergence of Celtic was the notion of mutual self-help:

> Though Celtic emerged as a result of a number of factors, one was this need to establish a welfare system for the Catholic Irish-Scots. Community pride was an important element in this decision. Spokesmen for the community explicitly discussed the need for them to show that they could look after themselves, to demonstrate that they were not a drain on the wider community's resources, and to stress their determination to make themselves part of Scottish society. (Finn, 1991: pp. 388–389)

In terms of the share issue, one interpretation of the willingness of supporters to subscribe for shares and the resultant exclusion of outside institutional shareholders is that it reflects continuing "community pride" or the desire of the community to continue demonstrating their ability to "look after themselves"[4]. Related to this is the link between Celtic (supporters) and the Catholic Church (Murray, 1984: p. 60; O'Hagan, 1999: p. 12). Bradley (1995: p. 61) found that an extraordinary 93% of Celtic supporters are Catholic. Furthermore a large majority of Celtic fans (61%) indicated that they attend church/mass at least once per week, a higher proportion than for the Catholic population as a whole and substantially higher than the figure reported at any other Scottish club (Bradley, 1995: p. 62). Given that evidence suggests that Catholics have shown greater loyalty to their church than members of other faiths (ONS, 1999: p. 220), it is possible that the club's supporters identified loyalty to Celtic (in terms of subscription for shares) as an extension of their loyalty to the Catholic Church.

As was mentioned previously, Celtic's traditional support was drawn from Irish immigrants in Glasgow, immigrants who for the most part were employed in unskilled, poorly paid jobs (Gallagher, 1987, p.61). Over time, however, this has changed with Murray (1998: p. 208) noting that "by the 1960s the success of Scotland's Catholic football club was paralleled by the success of Scottish Catholics throughout the business and professional world". In economic terms, therefore, many Celtic supporters would have been no less able than supporters of other clubs to afford to subscribe for shares in their club. Furthermore, football supporters in general are being drawn from a higher earnings background than was previously the case (SNCCFR, 1997).

Fergus McCann arrived at Celtic with a five-year plan, at the end of which he promised to sell his shareholding in the club and return to Bermuda. For some time he has indicated that his preferred option for selling his stake in the club has been to offer those shares for sale among the club's existing shareholders, season ticket holders and other investors interested in the long-term success of the club. At November 1998, ownership of the club was divided as shown in Table 2.

Table 2: Ownership of Celtic plc

Shareholder / Group	Percentage holding
Fergus McCann	50.3%
Supporters	40.0%
Dermot Desmond (non-executive director)	5.0%
John Keane (club director)	3.7%
Other directors and institutional investors	1.0%

Source: *The Scotsman* 11 November 1998

McCann's proposal is interesting, because it is the first time in the new business of football that supporters have been offered the opportunity to own a major British club in their own right (i.e. not beholden to a majority shareholder such as Fergus McCann, irrespective of whether that majority shareholder is also a supporter). This has implications with regard to the governance of Celtic, as two of the club's most important stakeholders, the supporters and the providers of capital, will become synonymous. It is also interesting because it almost certainly involves an unprecedented degree of altruism or philanthropy on the part of McCann. Recognised investment logic would indicate that the sale of a majority holding as a single stake would be worth far more to the seller than any sale which would involve a wide dispersal of that holding, given that the single buyer would be prepared to pay a premium for control.

Can such a transfer of shares to the supporters work? At present approximately 10,500 supporters already own shares in the club. If the argument is accepted that for most of these supporters the nature of this investment is essentially non-financial, i.e. it is of the nature of a community or an emotional investment (see also later section on Why be a Stock Exchange listed company?), then it is perhaps unlikely that many of these same supporters will wish to subscribe for additional shares. Unlike financial investors who gain from owning additional shares by receiving additional dividends and/or the benefit of share price movements, it might be argued that emotional investors do not receive additional benefits by holding additional shares, i.e. the emotional rights attached to owning say a hundred shares are no different or greater than those attached to owning one share. However, while 10,500 is a very large number of supporter-shareholders, nevertheless it equates to only approximately 20% of the club's season ticket holders, and to a much smaller percentage still of the club's world-wide supporter base. While the club may have its roots in Glasgow's Irish Catholic community, many of those roots have flourished far away from Glasgow.

The evidence of participation by the existing supporter-shareholders also bodes well for a successful transfer of McCann's shares. Despite being minority shareholders in a company controlled by its Chairman, attendance at the Celtic plc AGM in September 1998 was estimated at between 2,500 and 3,500, with the meeting lasting almost three hours (McLeman and Shand, 1998). It is also interesting to note that approximately 1600 (mostly small) shareholders attended Manchester United's 1998 AGM (Michie, 1998). By way of contrast, attendance at the AGMs of most public limited companies is very low. Such low attendances are explained by the fact that the diversified ownership prevalent in most UK companies, combined with the privileged access to information afforded to large institutional shareholders, means that there is little incentive for small shareholders to devote much attention to the monitoring and control of a company (Branston, Cowling, Duch Brown, Michie and Sugden, 1999; Jenkinson and Mayer, 1992). Given this, it can be argued that the AGM no longer provides a means for achieving shareholder democracy (Tricker, 1997). Attendance figures at the Celtic and Manchester United AGMs, however, somewhat conflict with this view of the role of the AGM. These levels of attendance are perhaps further evidence that supporter-shareholders do not think of themselves simply as minority owners of financial assets. Instead they see themselves as genuine stakeholders in the club, with rights both to receive information and to impart it to what they perceive as being their agents, namely the directors[5] .

Some, however, were not in favour of a scheme which would allow the supporters the opportunity to own their own club. A high profile consortium, led by the former Celtic legend Kenny Dalglish and the former singer with the rock group Simple Minds Jim Kerr, and backed by BT Capital Partners Europe, put forward an alternative strategy to takeover Celtic (Boyle, *et al.*, forthcoming), although no formal bid was made for McCann's shares. Perhaps the most interesting thing about the consortium has been not its proposals, but instead the way in which its activities have been reported in the (football) press and media. While little analysis has taken place of McCann's proposals, much of the media was quick to champion the consortium's case, despite the fact that it would have seen shares being placed with City institutions and financiers. It is difficult to avoid the conclusion that much of the sports media were influenced more by the presence of high profile personalities in the consortium, than any serious attempt to consider the issue of ownership of Celtic. While the celebrities used their high profile to influence journalists and reporters, in turn those journalists and reporters used their column inches and broadcasts to influence the supporters. Much of the press reporting of the consortium's bid was an example of what Rowe (1991: p. 88) describes as sports journalism "being embedded in, rather than illuminating its subject".

Why be a Stock Exchange listed company?

In the light of the above comments it is worth asking one further question: should such a community resource be a Stock Exchange listed company at all? In other words, are there not more appropriate organisational forms for football clubs such as Celtic?

The Stock Exchange is usually described as acting as both a primary market and as a secondary market. In strict terms, the Exchange is itself a secondary market. However, its existence makes the issue of new securities, which can subsequently be traded, a more attractive proposition.

The ostensible rationale for football clubs seeking Stock Exchange listings has been to raise funds for ground developments, although other reasons put forward in prospectuses issued by British football clubs include the strengthening of playing squads, development of commercial operations, investment in youth training programmes, widening share ownership, widening supporter share ownership, providing increased liquidity to shareholders, reduction of borrowings and the provision of additional working capital. The need to fund stadium developments is also one of the reasons why German clubs have pressurised the Deutsche Fussball-Bund (German Football Federation) to allow them to seek market listings (Bowley, 1998). Football club flotations which have raised substantial capital for ground developments include those at Manchester United, Bolton Wanderers, Charlton Athletic and Preston. Many football clubs, however, floated in 1996–97, after their grounds had been redeveloped as a consequence of the Taylor Report, redevelopment for which they received substantial public money (Football Task Force, 1999).

Advocating a structure other than that of a Stock Exchange listed company obviously restricts the ability of clubs to raise funds from that source for future capital investment. For football clubs this may not be as great a problem as it might first appear. First, irrespective of how it was funded, ground redevelopment at most major clubs is now complete. Second, football clubs are independent local companies, that independence being required by the rules of the football authorities which restrict the extent to which any person or persons can own shares in more than one club at the same time. The presence of these rules thus restricts the possibility of football clubs making corporate acquisitions of the sort found in more conventional business activity (i.e. takeovers of similar businesses). Therefore, given the absence at most clubs of a need for funding for either large scale capital investment or for corporate acquisitions, one argument is that clubs should seek organisational forms which are free from the pressure and conflicts that arise out of a Stock Exchange listing and which will at the same time encourage them to operate on a sustainable financial basis.

Conn (1997: p. 172) suggests another reason for club flotations, namely allowing the clubs' directors to make large capital gains on their original investment in the clubs. Interestingly in the case of Celtic it can be argued that this is not the case. The share issue in January 1995 was not accompanied by a market listing and involved only the sale of new shares, with no reduction in the holdings of the principal shareholder Fergus McCann. Furthermore, it can be argued that his decision to offer his majority holding to supporters and season-book holders, rather than selling it as a majority shareholding, will earn him a lesser return than if he had taken the decision to sell his stake as a controlling shareholding to one bidder. However, it should also be noted that Mr McCann will still make a very healthy return on his investment. It is also worth remembering that the majority of shares in Celtic were bought up by its supporters, as opposed to those groups who might normally be expected to provide capital in the market setting, i.e. City institutions.

The share issue took place in January 1995. The shares were accepted for listing on AIM in September 1995, before becoming listed on the main market in September 1998. In its role as a secondary market the Stock Exchange exists to provide a market where shares can be traded throughout their lives. The level of trading that takes place in shares depends on many factors — the company, the time of the year, market sentiment etc. Nevertheless there is evidence that shares in several football clubs are very thinly traded (Morrow, 1999, pp. 98–103). In the case of Celtic plc, Tables 3 and 4 indicate that there is very little evidence of trading taking place in its shares.

Table 3 shows the turnover in Celtic plc shares prior to the share split in September 1998. However, it must be noted that the figures have been adjusted for subsequent

Table 3:   Trading volume in Celtic plc shares (15 May 1997–16 September 1998)

Volume measure	Daily average	Details
Number of trades	4.67	The total number of times shares were traded in the day, as recorded by SEAQ.
Turnover by volume	7,037	The number of shares traded for a stock on a particular day.
Turnover by volume as a percentage of number of shares in issue	0.02%	
Turnover by value	£18,459	Average daily trading volume multiplied by adjusted price (adjusted for subsequent capital actions)
Number of shares in issue	29,000,000	

Source: Datastream, Company accounts

capital changes (i.e. these figures are as if the 100 for 1 share split that took place on 21 September 1998 had already taken place).

Notwithstanding that the figures in Table 3 are reported after adjustment for subsequent capital actions, the level of trading was based on the share capital prior to the share split. Prior to the split there were only 290,000 shares in issue, of which just over half were held by Fergus McCann, with the quoted price of these shares being measured in hundreds of pounds. It could be argued, therefore, that the extremely low levels of trading reported in Celtic shares may have been caused by two factors: first, the high price of those shares, and second, the low number of shares in issue.

Prior to its admittance to the Official List the club carried out a 100 for 1 share split. One of the motives behind share splits is to increase the liquidity and marketability of the company's shares. Table 4 shows the turnover in Celtic plc shares subsequent to the share split and the listing of Celtic shares on the Official List.

Table 4:   *Trading volume in Celtic plc shares (21 Sept. 1998 — 8 April 1999)*

Volume measure	Daily average
Number of bargains	14.1
Turnover by volume	14,717
Turnover by volume as a percentage of number of shares in issue	0.05%
Turnover by value	£46,522

Source: London Stock Exchange Electronic Data Services, Company accounts

As would be expected, higher turnover figures are reported for the latter period. However, the figures reported are still extremely low compared to other companies. In addition, higher trading might have been expected given the presence of a predatory consortium during that period. For comparative purposes, Table 5 shows trading volume data for the same period for three other leisure companies, including the football sector's red chip stock, Manchester United.

Taken together, Tables 3 and 4 indicate that shares in Celtic plc are extremely thinly traded. It has been suggested that the majority of supporters who bought shares in Celtic plc as a result of the public offer invested for community or emotional reasons rather than financial reasons, i.e. the supporters are interested in psychic income rather than financial income. Given this profile of shareholders, the turnover figures are unsurprising. The evidence does, however, further beg the question of why a company such as Celtic should be a Stock Exchange listed company at all.

Table 5:   *Trading volumes in leisure shares: daily averages (21 September 1998 — 8 April 1999)*

	Number of trades	Turnover by volume	Turnover by volume as a percentage of number of shares in issue	Turnover by value
Manchester United	49.0	628,438	0.25%	£1,349,158
Rank	132.3	2,715,349	0.35%	£5,973,814
Ladbroke	268.1	5,812,489	0.49%	£12,883,610

Source: Datastream, Company accounts

Other organisational forms

As was mentioned previously, the philosophical antecedents of stakeholder theory can be traced to the conceptions of the co-operative movement and mutuality. In this section the appropriateness of mutual and co-operative ownership structures to contemporary football clubs will be briefly considered. (For a more detailed discussion of alternative ownership models see Bourke, 1999; Branston et al., 1999; Michie, 1999; Michie and Ramalingam, 1999).

Mutuality

Recent discussion on mutuality has primarily focused on its demise in the financial services sector, as witnessed by the high profile demutualisation of many building societies and more recently of life assurance providers such as Scottish Widows. While the demise of mutuality in the financial services sector mirrors earlier decline in other sectors such as the retail market, mutuals and co-operatives continue to provide a significant share of the services we rely on most such as childcare, insurance, food provision and agriculture (Leadbeater and Christie, 1999). Thus while the nature of the financial services industry may mean that mutuality is no longer appropriate for all providers in that market, equally there has been a realisation in other areas of activity that new forms of mutual structure may be appropriate where the primary aim of the product or activity is not to generate a financial return or where a community need is being met (Jaquiss, 2000). As Michie (1999) notes, structuring football clubs as mutual organisations seems to be particularly appropriate given that a club can be defined in economic terms (using the 1996 definition by Cornes and Sandler) as:

... a voluntary group of individuals who derive mutual benefit from sharing
one or more of the following: production costs, the members' characteristics,
or a good characterised by excludable benefits (cited in Michie, 1999, p.17)

In a mutual business, ownership is achieved through active participation in the
business. The members are the owners and have voting rights, but no tradeable
financial asset exists. Many sporting clubs continue to be run as mutual organisations,
with Barcelona being perhaps the most prominent example. Barcelona is a not-for-
profit association owned by its 104,000 members. Any surplus made is reinvested
directly into the club. Three other Spanish clubs, Real Madrid, Athletico Bilbao and
Osasuna also operate as not-for-profit associations. Mutual sports organisations also
have a long history in other countries, notably Germany, although it should be noted
that German football clubs have recently received approval from the Deutsche
Fussball-Bund (DFB) to allow them to drop their mutual status and become publicly
listed companies. This change reflects an acceptance by the DFB of the German clubs'
argument that they needed access to stock markets in order to allow them to compete
on equal terms with their European rivals.

In the case of a football club, ownership would be conferred on the club's active
supporters. With no outside shareholders, any surplus or profit made can be reinvested
in the club. In this way one of the most prominent stakeholder conflicts which exists
within listed football clubs, namely the tension between supporters and providers of
financial capital, is effectively eliminated.

Michie and Ramalingam (1999) identify benefits of the mutual form, two of which
are of particular relevance to football clubs: first, that mutuality is a more efficient way
of dealing with agency problems, and second, that mutuality is a source of social
welfare.

In a mutual, agency problems are resolved by the fact that as members can simply
withdraw their funds this acts as a discipline on management. However, the loyalty of
supporters makes the exercising of such 'exit' discipline unlikely (Michie and
Ramalingam, 1999). The nature of football club investment, as discussed throughout
this paper, and in particular as evidenced in the low levels of trading reported in shares
in Celtic plc, backs up this view that supporters are unlikely to exercise such exit
discipline (see also McMaster, 1997, and Morrow, 1999: p. 88). However, instead of
exit discipline it is argued that what is described as the power of 'voice' could act as
an equally rigorous discipline on management (Michie and Ramalingam, 1999).
Evidence presented earlier in this paper as to the levels of attendance and participation
at football club AGMs provides some credence for this argument[6]. The power of
'voice' at present, however, is limited within many modern football corporations. What
mutual status may provide is an opportunity for the 'voice' to become more effective
in the governance process by ensuring that it is heard within a more democratic
structure[7].

With regard to social relationships, it is argued that mutual forms of ownership can be advantageous in that such businesses (building societies being the obvious example) are better able to sustain long term relationships with customers (Michie and Ramalingam, 1999). Given that the relationship between a supporter and his or her club is essentially an issue of identity and is therefore a long-term relationship, it can be argued that the mutual form of ownership is thus very appropriate for football clubs.

In practice, however, given the market capitalisation of many top clubs (including Celtic), it may be difficult to convert Stock Exchange listed companies into mutuals. However, evidence presented in this paper suggests that many Celtic shareholders do not view their shareholding as a financial investment in any conventional sense. If other like-minded supporters were to subscribe for those shares presently held by Fergus McCann, then conversion to mutual status may not be entirely unrealistic. Furthermore, the exchange of shares for ownership or membership of their club is likely to be more palatable to football club shareholders than to conventional shareholders: altruism is not the sole preserve of Fergus McCann. Nevertheless, the practical difficulties of such a conversion, not least how it would be financed, should not be underestimated — the best route to becoming a mutual is unlikely to begin at a plc structure[8].

An alternative and perhaps more practicable way of allowing supporters to exercise their 'voice' is through part of a club's share capital being held by a Trust on behalf of the supporters. Such trusts already exist at Bournemouth and Northampton Town[9]. Trusts preserve the principle of mutuality as they provide for the sharing of the ownership of property and operate on a one-member one-vote basis. One reaction to the decision by the Secretary of State for Trade and Industry to block BSkyB's bid for Manchester United was an announcement by the campaign group Supporters United Against Murdoch (SUAM) that it intended to seek a meeting with the Manchester United plc board to discuss the possibility of setting up some kind of trust to combine the holding of individual fans (Crick, 1999). To that end SUAM also advised its members to go out and buy as many shares in the club as they can.

Co-operatives

An alternative organisational form, also based on the principle of mutuality, is that of the co-operative. A co-operative can be defined as "an autonomous association of persons united voluntarily to meet their common economic, social, and cultural needs and aspirations through a jointly owned and democratically controlled enterprise" (ICA, 1996). Co-operatives are characterised by:

- mutuality — conduct of the business must be for the mutual benefit of the members, with the benefits they receive deriving mainly from their participation in the business;

- the principle of one member, one vote — control of the co-operative must be vested in the members equally;
- fair distribution of profits — profits, if distributable, will be distributed in relation to the extent members have either traded with the co-operative or taken part in its business.

The aim of a co-operative is to ensure a genuine community interest among the co-operative's members, with that interest being based on something deeper than the amount of financial capital they have placed in that organisation (Bourke, 1999). The nature and importance of a football club's community (both direct and indirect) was discussed earlier in this paper. A club's community is vital to its future success. Adoption of a co-operative structure would introduce democracy into football clubs, i.e. it would provide all of a club's members (or stakeholders) with a say in the running of the club. Thus it would ensure that those who are most important to the club's future long-term success, its supporters and also its players, are actively involved in running their club and planning its future. Interestingly, sports (including professional football clubs) were identified in Tuck's 1981 typology of industries and services most suitable for co-operative development (cited in Clarke, 1984).

It is important to highlight the fact that running a football club as a co-operative does not mean that it would not be run as a business. The important distinction between a co-operative and a non-cooperative is what happens to the profits made by that business: while profits in a non-cooperative would be distributed to shareholders, in a co-operative where the objectives of the members are defined in terms of footballing objectives, those profits would be retained in the co-operative.

The experience of plc co-operatives in the Irish dairy industry may be informative for football clubs. One argument in favour of Stock Exchange listing as opposed to co-operative or mutual status is that it makes it easier to raise capital. Faced with the problem of requiring to raise capital to fund modernisation and expansion in a competitive market place, while wishing also to maintain co-operative ownership by their farmer-suppliers, the dairy co-operatives adopted a hybrid structure of co-operative plc status. This involved the creation of Stock Exchange quoted subsidiaries with full plc status but which remained under the control of the members of the co-operatives (Bourke, 1999). The challenge for football clubs would be to reach the same point but from the other direction, i.e. to move from a corporate structure in which control is vested in the hands of one or a few individuals or institutional shareholders, to one which allows the club's supporters (who are equivalent to the farmers) to assume control. However, as was mentioned in the discussion on mutuality, the practical difficulties of such a conversion, not least its financing, should not be underestimated.

Conclusion

Football clubs are classic stakeholder organisations. Various groups other than a club's shareholders believe that de facto they have ownership rights in their club. Conflicts between stakeholders, however, are likely, particularly between supporters (who may or may not also be shareholders) whose objectives are essentially in terms of football and shareholders (professional investors) who to a large extent are motivated by the prospect of a financial return. Such conflicts have been apparent at several clubs, most noticeably at Manchester United and Newcastle United, and might be thought of as inevitable where a club becomes a Stock Exchange listed company.

In this paper, however, the case of Stock Exchange listed Celtic plc has been used, not to demonstrate conflict between stakeholders, but instead to question the appropriateness of market listing for contemporary football clubs. In the case of Celtic there already exists a high degree of overlap between the stakeholder groups of supporters and shareholders, with the potential to further increase this overlap in the near future. One consequence arising out of this ownership framework is that very little trading takes place in shares in Celtic plc. Although this lack of market activity is unsurprising, it provides further evidence that Stock Exchange listed companies are not the most appropriate vehicles for contemporary stakeholder-focused football clubs. What is required for football clubs is a structure which more fully captures both the economic and the social aspects of contemporary football clubs and allows for a more inclusive concept of ownership. While mutual and co-operative structures have much to commend them, given the market value of many top clubs, the most practicable way forward is likely to involve the formation of supporters' trusts operating on mutual principles within the existing corporate structure.

Postscripts

1.   Subsequent to this paper, supporters' trusts have been launched at a number of British clubs. The background to the setting up of the Celtic Trust can be found in Carr, P., Findlay, J., Hamil, S., Hill, J. and Morrow, S. (2001) 'The Celtic Trust', *Soccer and Society*, Vol. 1, No. 3: pp. 70–87.

2.   Despite a minimum investment of £700 being required, subscriptions were received for just over 75% of Feargus McCann's shares, generating a sum of just over £20m. At April 2001, Celtic has approximately 16,000 shareholders who between them own approximately 45% of the company.

Acknowledgement

A version of this paper has been published in *The Irish Accounting Review*, Vol. 7, No. 2, pp. 61–90.

Notes

[1] Restrictions on the mobility of football players arising out of the operation of the football transfer system were challenged by a Belgian player, Jean Marc Bosman, in an action raised against his club and the footballing authorities. In a landmark ruling the Court of Justice of the European Communities held that the provision that out-of-contract football players could only move between two clubs if compensation was paid to the selling club was incompatible with Article 48 of the EC Treaty (CJEC, 1995). (For a more detailed consideration of the case, see Griffith-Jones, 1997, pp. 126–133 or Morris, Morrow and Spink, 1996.)

[2] See Michie (1998) for evidence of stakeholder dissatisfaction with the bid.

[3] During the year ended 30 June 1998, the Celtic Charity Fund raised over £120,000 to be distributed among worthy causes (Celtic plc 1998 Annual Report).

[4] The link between the incoming Irish and the idea of mutual self-help evidences itself elsewhere. For example, Donnelly and Haggert (1997) identify the influence of the Irish in Scotland as being one reason why the Credit Union movement has been so much more successful in Scotland than in England and Wales. In terms of political beliefs, evidence also suggests that Celtic fans continue to be supporters of the Labour Party to a significantly larger extent than fans of any other Scottish club (Bradley, 1995: p. 69).

[5] The determination of small supporter-shareholders to participate in the operation of their club was well illustrated at the Celtic plc 1998 AGM. Notwithstanding the existence of an individual majority shareholder, numerous shareholders spoke against an apparently uncontroversial resolution (common in most public limited companies) that the directors should be allowed to disapply statutory pre-emption rights in respect of allotment of shares for cash, before forcing a vote on the issue.

[6] The importance of 'voice' was evident at the Celtic plc 1998 AGM, attended by approximately 2500 shareholders (McLeman and Shand, 1998). Reports in the Scottish broadsheet press included descriptions such as 'a tempestuous agm', 'sustained abuse', 'McCann who was also the subject of barracking as well as receiving a standing ovation', 'pandemonium at Celtic Park' and 'Democracy … in football is not a pretty sight'. (See for example 'Brown defies calls to quit', 'McCann and Brown cast as villains in Parkhead melodrama', The Scotsman, 15 September 1998).

[7] Mutuality does not, however, guarantee democracy. For example, L'Elefant Blau, an organisation set up by members of FC Barcelona, has as its primary goal the democratisation of FC Barcelona. Among other things it is critical of the process by which the members entitled to attend the Assembly of Delegates (the highest government body of the

club) are selected, and of the accountability of the club's directors to its members (L'Elefant Blau, 1999).

8   For a discussion on the feasibility of applying the mutual concept in practice, see Michie (1999: p. 19).

9   At the 1999 Labour Party conference the Secretary of State for Culture, Media and Sport, the Rt. Hon. Chris Smith MP announced a Government initiative to help give supporters a say in the running of their football clubs by forming mutual trusts. Supporters Direct was subsequently launched in January 2000 to provide assistance to supporters who wish to form trusts.

References

Ansoff, I. (1987) *Corporate strategy*. Harmondsworth: Middlesex: Penguin Books.

Arnold, A. and Benveniste, I. (1987) 'Wealth and poverty in the English Football League', *Accounting and Business Research*, Vol. 17, No. 67: pp. 195–203.

Bourke, A. (1999) 'The evolution of Irish Plc Co-operatives — lessons for English football clubs', in S. Hamil, J. Michie and C. Oughton (eds) *A game of two halves? The business of football*. Edinburgh: Mainstream, pp. 180–194.

Bowley, G. (1998) 'Clubs push for stock market flotation', *The Financial Times*, Survey: p. 7, 24 June.

Boyle, R. Dinan, W. and Morrow, S. (forthcoming) 'Doing the business? the newspaper reportin of the business of football'.

Bradley, J.M. (1995) *Ethnic and religious identity in modern Scotland: Culture, politics and football*. Aldershot: Avebury.

Branston, R., Cowling, K., Duch Brown, N., Michie, J. and Sugden, R. (1999) 'Modern corporations and the public interest', in S. Hamil, J. Michie and C. Oughton (eds) *A game of two halves? The business of football*. Edinburgh: Mainstream, pp. 180–194.

CJEC (1995) Judgement of the Court-Union Royale Belge des Sociètès de Football Association ASBL v Bosman. Case C-415/93. 15 December. (Court of Justice of the European Communities).

Clarke, T. (1984) 'Alternative modes of co-operative production', *Economic and Industrial Democracy*, Vol. 5: pp. 97–129.

—— (1998) 'The stakeholder corporation: A business philosophy for the information age', *Long Range Planning*, Vol. 21, No. 2: pp. 182–194.

Conn, D. (1997) *The football business — fair game in the '90s?*. Edinburgh: Mainstream.

Crick, M. (1999) '1–0 to the SUAM as BSkyB takeover is blocked', *The Daily Telegraph*: p. 3, April 10.

Deloitte & Touche (1998) *Annual review of football finance*. Manchester: Deloitte & Touche.

Donnelly, R. and Haggert, A. (1997) *Credit Unions in Britain — a decade of growth*. Oxford: Plunkett Foundation.

L'Elefant Blau, (1999) 'The struggle for democracy at Barcelona FC', in S. Hamil, J. Michie and C. Oughton (eds) *A game of two halves? The business of football*. Edinburgh: Mainstream, pp. 202–208.

Finn, G.P.T. (1991) 'Racism, religion and social prejudice: Irish Catholic clubs, soccer and Scottish society — II social identities and conspiracy theories', *International Journal of Sports History*, Vol. 8, Part 3: pp. 370–397.

Football Task Force (1999) *Football: Commercial issues. A submission by The Football Task Force to the Minister for Sport*. 22 December 1999.

Freeman, R. (1984) *Strategic management: A stakeholder approach*. Boston: Pitman.

Gallagher. T. (1987) *Glasgow — the uneasy peace*. Manchester: Manchester University Press.

Griffith-Jones, D. (1997) *Law and the business of sport*. London: Butterworths.

Hamil, S. (1999) 'A whole new ball game? Why football needs a regulator', in S. Hamil, J. Michie and C. Oughton (eds) *A game of two halves? The business of football*. Edinburgh: Mainstream, pp. 23–39.

Hutton, W. (1995) *The state we're in*. London: Jonathan Cape.

ICA (1996) International Co-operative Information Centre, International Co-operative Alliance (available at http://www.wisc.edu/uwcc/icic).

Jaquiss, K. (2000) 'Football, fans and fat cats: Whose football club is it anyway?', in Hamil, S., Michie, J., Oughton, C. and Warby, S. (eds) *Football in the digital age: Whose game is it anyway?*. Edinburgh: Mainstream, pp. 112–117.

Jenkinson, T. and Mayer, C. (1992) 'The assessment: Corporate governance and corporate control', *Oxford Review of Economic Policy*, Vol. 8, No. 3: pp. 1–10.

Kay, J. (1993) *Foundations of corporate success*. Oxford: Oxford University Press.

King, A. (1997) 'New directors, customers and fans: The transformation of English football in the 1990s', *Sociology of Sport Journal*, Vol. 14: pp. 224–240.

Leadbeater, C. and Christie, I. (1999) *To our mutual advantage*. London: Demos.

Lee, S. (1999) 'The BSkyB Bid for Manchester United plc', in S. Hamil, J. Michie and C. Oughton (eds) *A game of two halves? The business of football*. Edinburgh: Mainstream, pp. 82–111,

McLeman, N. and Shand, D. (1998) 'Brown defies calls to quit', *The Scotsman*, 15 September: p. 34.

McMaster, R. (1997) 'The market for corporate control in professional football: Is there an agency problem?', *Economic Affairs*, Vol. 17, No. 3: September, pp. 25–29.

Michie, J. (1998) 'United against Murdoch', *Tribune*, 30 November.

——— (1999) *New mutualism: A golden goal?*. London: The Co-operative Party.

Michie, J. and Ramalingam, S. (1999) 'Whose game is it anyway? Shareholders, mutuals and trusts', in S. Hamil, J. Michie and C. Oughton (eds) *A game of two halves? The business of football.* Edinburgh: Mainstream, pp. 158–167.

Morris, P.E., Morrow, S. and Spink: P. (1996) 'EC law and professional football: Bosman and its implications', *Modern Law Review*, Vol. 59, No. 6: pp. 893–902.

Morrow, S. (1997a) 'Accounting for football players. Financial and accounting implications of "Royal Club Liègois and others versus Bosman" for football in the United Kingdom', *Journal of Human Resource Costing and Accounting*, Vol. 2, No. 1: pp. 55–71.

——— (1997b) 'The City's match of the day', *New Economy*, Vol. 4, No. 4: pp. 202–206.

——— (1999) *The new business of football: Accountability and finance in football.* Basingstoke: Macmillan.

Murray, B. (1984) *The old firm: Sectarianism, sport and society in Scotland.* Edinburgh: John Donald Publishers.

——— (1998) *The old firm in the new age: Celtic and Rangers since the Souness revolution.* Edinburgh: Mainstream.

O'Hagan, A. (1999) 'The final whistle for God's squad?', *The Guardian*, 27 February, pp. 8–15.

ONS (1999) *Social Trends 1999 edition.* London: Office for National Statistics.

Perryman, M. (1998) *Football United: New Labour, the task force and the future of the game.* London: The Fabian Society.

Roberts, R.W. (1998) 'A stakeholder approach to the corporate single audit', *Critical Perspectives on Accounting*, Vol. 9, No. 2: pp. 227–232.

Rowe, D. (1991) 'That misery of Stringer's clichès: Sports writing', *Cultural Studies*, Vol. 5, January: pp. 77–90.

RSA (1995) *Tomorrow's company: The role of business in a changing world.* London: The Royal Society for the Encouragement of Arts, Commerce and Manufactures.

Sloane: P. (1971) 'The economics of professional football: The football club as a utility maximiser', *Scottish Journal of Political Economy*, June: pp. 121–146.

——— (1980) *Sport in the market, Hobart Paper Number 85.* London: Institute of Economic Affairs.

Smith, Sir John (1997) *Football — its values, finances and reputation. Report to the Football Association by Sir John Smith.* London: The Football Association Limited.

SNCCFR (1997) *FA Premier League Fan Surveys 1996/97 General Sample Report.* University of Leicester: Sir Norman Chester Centre for Football Research.

Sternberg, E. (1998) *Corporate Governance*: Accountability in the Marketplace. London: The Institute of Economic Affairs.

Stewart, G. (1986) 'The retain and transfer system: An alternative perspective', *Managerial Finance*, Vol. 12, No. 1: pp. 25–29.

Sutherland, R.J. and Haworth, M. (1986) 'The economics of the industry', *Managerial Finance*, Vol. 12, No. 1: pp. 1–5.

Tricker, B. (1997) 'Information and power — The influence of IT on corporate gxovernance', *Corporate Governance*, Vol. 5, Part 2: pp. 49–51.

Wilson, B. (1988) *Celtic: A century with honour*. London: William Collins Sons & Co. Ltd.

Centres and Peripheries:
An Historical Perspective on the Diffusion of Leisure Practices in Rural Nineteenth Century Scotland

Lorna Jackson
University of Edinburgh

Introduction

The geographical concept of centre and periphery is one which, applied to cultural studies, lends itself to an examination of cultural diffusion — the processes and mechanisms by which changing cultural practices spread through a society. Social historians of sport have debated the merits of a social downward diffusion model, particularly in relation to the spread of codified institutionalised sport from the English public schools (Walvin, 1978; Dunning and Sheard, 1979; Mangan, 1983); whereas the limitations of such a model have been clearly identified by, among others, Vamplew (1988), Mason (1988), Bailey (1989), Holt (1989), and Lowerson (1994). Tranter (1998) has cogently summarised the position, noting how "the social diffusionist interpretation of sport's dispersal obscures the influence exerted by distance, community size and, particularly, cultural boundaries" (Tranter, 1998: p. 30). Bale's work on the spatial dispersal of professional football (Bale, 1978) suggested a ripple effect model to account for the diffusion of sporting change — the greater the distance from the epicentre of the innovation, the later its adoption.

To what extent is this simpler model valid if applied beyond sport to a broader range of cultural practices, or to an area which itself is peripheral? What were the mechanisms by which cultural innovations were spread, and can any consistent pattern be identified in a particular geographical locality? Did sporting activities follow a different pattern of diffusion from social or improving activities, and to what extent do local demographic, economic and cultural forces influence the process?

This paper addresses such issues by focusing on a case study of a peripheral county of rural nineteenth century Scotland.

The context

The national context may have been one of industrialisation, urbanisation and rapid social change in the cities and Central Lowlands of Scotland (Bailey, 1978; Ferguson, 1978; Cunningham, 1980; Clarke and Critcher, 1985; Fraser and Morris, 1990; Lynch, 1991), but in the more remote parts of the nation the pace of change was less rapid. Geographically and culturally, Argyll's identity is aligned with the Highlands, with a deeply indented coastline which made the sea the natural highway and a history which gave the ethnic background to modern Scotland. Even by mid-nineteenth century the county was still predominantly rural, with only minor small local industries based on the exploitation of natural resources. Population had peaked in 1831 at 101,000 and thereafter it seeped away in a slow and steady decline to 73,500 by 1901.

Settlement was scattered, because of the nature of the land, and in island communities, steamer services with the mainland provided the link to the outside world: thus Tobermory and Salen in Mull were linked with Oban, Port Ellen and Bowmore in Islay with Crinan. Campbeltown at the foot of the long Kintyre peninsula had regular connections with Ayr and with Greenock, and daily steamer services also ran from Greenock through the Kyles of Bute and up Loch Fyne to Ardrishaig, the terminus of the Crinan Canal which linked with the west coast and avoided the stormy Mull of Kintyre. From Crinan, at the other end of the canal, a steamer connection ran to Oban, thence Fort William and the North. Small market towns, such as Campbeltown, Tarbert and Lochgilphead on the mainland, served local populations, as did larger villages on the principal islands. There were industrial villages at Easdale, Luing and Ballachulish quarrying slate; at Taynuilt, Bonawe and Furnace quarrying granite; while gunpowder was manufactured at Furnace, Millhouse near Tighnabruaich and Kilmelford.

Land was the principal base of wealth and power, and the large estates which were the main pattern of landholding were generally still in the hands of the traditional local gentry — albeit those in more precarious financial positions were now letting out their estates to meet the growing demand for country sports (Cannadine, 1990; Jarvie, Jackson and Higgins, 1997). Estate workers lived in small communities, barely villages, and only in the more fertile parts of the county (south Kintyre and south Islay) was there substantial arable farming.

Thus the nature of this setting is very different from that of the industrial and urban settings to which much historical leisure research has been directed. To examine the processes of cultural diffusion, this study does not consider the traditional and persisting leisure activities such as shinty and other games and pastimes (Maclagan, 1901; Jackson, 1999a), but focuses on innovations in cultural pursuits which can be both identified and dated by reference to local newspapers and local archive material. There are obvious methodological limitations on the use of such sources, but they do provide some indication of the inception and spread of new sporting, improving and social activities across the county.

Argyll in the nineteenth century had a far greater number of remote communities than in the present time — small village settlements isolated from social contact with other communities except by water. The opening of the Crinan Canal in 1801, the building of the railway to Oban in 1880 and road improvements later in the century gradually improved communications outwith as well as within the county — but only for the sections of the population who could afford travel. Lacking mass media of communications, who were the innovators of cultural change, and from which centre or centres did diffusion occur?

Sport

"The game of golf is peculiar to the east of Scotland, but it never succeeded in getting a footing in the west". Thus wrote the editor of the *Campbeltown Courier* on 18 March 1876 reporting an innovation in the community: a meeting had been held for the purposes of organising a Golf Club in the town or its vicinity. Golf had been codified by the St Andrew's Society of Golfers (subsequently the Royal and Ancient) in 1754, although the first formally constituted golf club, The Company of Edinburgh Golfers, was founded at Leith in 1744 (Tranter, 1998: p. 14). The meeting at Campbeltown agreed that "the rules of golf in force at Prestwick should be adopted" and the course, of ten holes, was located to the west of the town at Machrihanish on land where "the farmer seems agreeable to our playing" (McDiarmid, 1976: p. 4). The gentlemen who promoted the club included a minister, two doctors, a banker, a local businessman and two Army Captains, both from the Militia then based in Campbeltown (*Campbeltown Courier*, 18 March 1876). With an entrance fee of five shillings and a similar annual subscription (McDiarmid, 1976: p. 4), the cost is clearly well below the five shillings a week cited by Holt for the suburban middle classes (Holt, 1998: p.77), but clearly these male members were not from the working classes. Machrihanish's connection with Prestwick continued when the course was extended to twelve holes by the Prestwick professional Charles Hunter; in 1879 Tom Morris of St Andrew's extended the course to eighteen holes to put the first tee within easier reach of the local village inn (McDiarmid, 1976: p. 5).

Later newspaper references make clear the extensive support of the local gentry, yet despite the fact that natural landscapes of the links type can be found in the Kintyre peninsula and elsewhere in Argyll, and that links golf used an essentially unaltered landscape (Price, 1989: p. 75; Bale, 1994: p. 54), the model of golf at Machrihanish was slow to spread (see Table 1). In some instances the significance of local gentry or sporting tenants' initiative is the key factor (Inverneill's personal course; Sopwith, the summer tenant on Lismore; Lord Archibald Campbell, the Duke of Argyll's son, on

Table 1   *First newspaper report of Golf courses in Argyll*

1876	Machrihanish
1889	Dunaverty; Southend
1890	Oban — Ganavan; moved to Glencruitten 1892
1891	Lochgilphead; Machrie, Port Ellen, Islay
1893	Taynuilt; Bonaw; Inveraray; Connel Ferry, Kilmelford
1894	Tighnabruaich; Inverneill (personal course for Landowner); Lismore
1895	Personal course in Oban (Pulpit Hill)
1896	Uisguintuie, Port Charlotte, Islay; Strachur; Kilnaughton, Oa, Islay; Tobermory — Erray; moved to Mishnish 1897
1897	Appin; Iona; Scarinish, Tiree
1898	Gigha; Tarbert

Sources: *Oban Times, Argyllshire Herald, Argyllshire Standard, Campbeltown Courier*

Table 2   *First newspaper reports of Cricket in Argyll*

1859	Campbeltown	(Inland Revenue)
1863	Inveraray	(Ducal family)
1867	Kilmartin	(Malcolm of Poltalloch)
	Lochgilphead	
	Oban	revived 1874; 1889
1868	Carradale	(Shooting tenant)
1878	Bridgend; Bowmore	
1879	Taynuilt; Bonawe	
1880	Lochbuy, Mull	
1885	Kilberry, Knapdale	(Campbell of Kilberry)
1890	Tarbert	(Campbell of Stonefield)
1891	Largie	(MacDonald of Largie)

Sources: *Oban Times, Argyllshire Herald, Argyllshire Standard, Campbeltown Courier*

Table 3   *First newspaper report of Glass Ball competitions in Argyll*

1880	Lochfyne Club (Ardrishaig)
1883	Kilmartin
1884	Dalmally
1885	Lochaweside
1887	Tarbert; Ardgour and Sunart
1889	Tighnabruaich
1890	Glencoe
1892	Lochgair
1893	Aharacle
1895	Kilmelford; Glenorchy; Easdale
1896	Inveraray

Sources: *Oban Times, Argyllshire Herald, Argyllshire Standard, Campbeltown Courier*

Tiree); elsewhere the course opened at Oban in 1890 spawned later a cluster of very local imitators at Taynuilt, Bonaw and Connel Ferry in 1883, which at the first two might have served the working men employed in the quarries there — an example of imitation or downward dissemination? The increasing popularity in the nineties does show some ripple effect with more island courses being opened later in the decade than the mainland courses of 1893/4. However as few of these courses survive, there is little evidence to explain the erratic and uneven pattern of development.

Cricket is another sporting newcomer to Argyll (see Table 2). The first report of its arrival is in the guise of the Campbeltown Civil Service Cricketing Club, a club for inland revenue officers (excisemen) associated with the town's distilleries (*Argyllshire Herald*, 23 June 1859). Opening its ranks to the town's gentlemen in the next season, the Campbeltown Cricket Club flourished through to the end of the century.

Campbeltown's early links were with clubs in Ayr — from 1868 playing on the day of the Kintyre Agricultural Society show in Campbeltown, to which special steamer excursions ran from Ayr, and with Glasgow. The composition of this club cannot be ascertained after its inception, but the link with the excisemen would seem to accord with Tranter's assessment of Stirlingshire cricket clubs as drawing from social class C (Tranter, 1998: p. 40). The Islay clubs of Bridgend and Bowmore are possibly linked with the excisemen of the distilleries there, or other incomers appointed to instruct the Volunteer forces (Jackson, 1999b). Similar working class composition might be found in the later clubs of Taynuilt and Bonawe, with local quarry communities. However other clubs in the county were more clearly linked with the elite, as indicated above, albeit the composition of the teams might on occasion include estate workers or other local artisans: but some were comprised solely of guests shooting on the estate involved. From newspaper reports, several of the patrons of these estate based teams had military as well as land-owning connections; for a number an English public school education is also a common factor. However, as there was little competition between the elite and working men's teams, the social diffusion model does not seem to apply, and imitation might explain some clubs although the ripple model is insufficient.

For another sport (see Table 3), the ripple pattern does seem to hold true — at least initially. Glass ball shooting was the nineteenth century version of clay pigeon shooting — the glass balls, fired from a trap, contained a feather so that when a bullet shattered the glass, the feather was visible floating down. The sport first appeared in Argyll at the Lochfyne Club, Ardrishaig in March 1880, and was held according to Bogardo's rules (*Oban Times*, 20 March 1880). By the following year it had segregated classes of entrants — gamekeepers, amateurs with gun licenses (i.e. gentlemen) and "all comers, including fishermen" (*Oban Times*, 2 April 1881). Thereafter it spread up country to the villages between Ardrishaig and Lochaweside, then south along the steamer route: was it the equipment that was being shared as well as the sport? At a later date Kilmelford's competition was run with "balls being sent from a strong new revolving trap which tried the powers of the competitors to the utmost' (*Oban Times*, 8 February 1896), so the sport required a high skill level. This doubtless explained the segregation of game-keepers in a class of their own — the professional shots could not be seen to compete with their employers, the land-owning gentlemen amateurs.

As well as Ardrishaig's status as a transport nexus (a steamer port and also the southern end of the Crinan Canal which connected with the west coast), nearby

Lochgilphead was the headquarters of the Administrative Battalion of the county's Volunteer forces. This may be a connecting factor, not only in the initial ripple spread but also in the later more erratic pattern: the network of Volunteer force detachments around the country would have welcomed the opportunity to practise their shooting skill, acquired through military training, in a sweepstakes competition. However, again the timing shows a pattern of uneven development.

What of football, the classic example of diffusion to the working classes of the modern, organised and codified game? The earliest references in Argyll to football seem to be to a traditional form of the game, which had been in decline by the 1860s although persisting in more remote areas in an unreconstructed form of prolonged duration and with large numbers of participants (Jackson 1999a: p. 38). From 1877 the references to clubs in the Oban area proliferate; in Campbeltown the Inland Revenue set up a football club in 1879, and 1880 saw the first reference to Association Rules in Bender-loch, north of Oban, where the laird had been promoting football as a substitute for the traditional New Year's day shinty since 1868. On 10 January 1880, for old New Year's day, Lochgilphead played Glasgow Lochgilphead — urban workers having returned for the major annual celebration to their home town. Thus there is clearly more than one mechanism by which the new sport is being spread — and with great success, judging by the proliferation over a relatively short time of village teams and local competitions. The participants are variously identified as fishermen, printers, agricultural workers, "working lads" and members of the Volunteer forces. (*Argyllshire Herald, Argyllshire Standard, Campbeltown Courier, Oban Times*, various dates). As popularity increased, Argyll formed its own Football Association in 1889, which prior to affiliation with the Scottish Football Association, ran an annual County cup competition, the final of which in its first two years was played at Ibrox Park, Govan and Cappielow Park, Greenock respectively (*Oban Times*: 29 March 1890, 7 March 1891). In this sport, the late uptake may indicate the county's peripheral position as compared with the spread of the game in more populous central areas; internally the pattern of diffusion is certainly more rapid than the other sports examined, but the mechanisms are complex.

The other great working class sport is notable by its absence, thus signalling Argyll's Highland rather than Lowland status — the sport of quoits. Despite Tranter's evidence on its popularity among the working classes (Tranter, 1989: p. 57), there are only sporadic instances of its occurrence in Argyll (see table 4). These are mostly communities with more industrial working class men than some of the remote rural settlements. The only instance which falls into the latter rather than the former category is that reported at Achnamara in Knapdale, where the game had been introduced by the workmen employed in building an estate house for Colonel Malcolm of Poltalloch, younger (*Argyllshire Standard*, 26 July 1884). It could be argued that cultural barriers (lack of knowledge or a visual model, or its non-traditionality) restricted the diffusion of this otherwise nationally popular sport. Again the pattern is uneven and slow in spread.

Table 4	First Newspaper reports of Quoits matches in Argyll
1859	Campbeltown
1872	Ardgour
1879	Taynuilt
1883	Lochgilphead
1884	Toward; Achnamara
1894	Bridgend, Islay
1896	Tarbert

Sources: *Oban Times, Argyllshire Herald, Argyllshire Standard, Campbeltown Courier*

Temperance and friendly societies

There is considerable evidence from the mid-century onwards that the respectable working classes of Argyll were sharing to some extent in a rise in disposable income, or in the social pressure to better conditions for one's family. From 1864 onwards there are increasing reports of the occurrence of friendly and temperance societies with objectives of either savings or temperance or both. Here the initiatives appear to have come primarily from the working classes themselves, although subscriptions may have come from patrons such as local landowners or paternalistic employers. The Independent Order of Good Templars movement entered Argyll by way of Campbeltown and spread rapidly in its early months by coastal lines — and by the naming of many of the branches, most likely through (see Table 5) the agency of the fishermen. Ardrishaig's Fishermen's Good Hope, Tarbert's Fishermen's Lifeboat, Oban's Galley

Table 5	First newspaper reports of Temperance societies in Argyll: Independent Order of Good Templars	
1871	Campbeltown	
	Ardrishaig	"Fishermen's ..."
	Lochgilphead;	
	Tarbert	"Fishermen's ...";
	Southend	
	Oban	"Galley ...
1872	Ballachulish	
	Tobermory	
	Glencoe	
	Bonaw	
1874	Inveraray	
1875	Kilbrandon	
	Tobermory 2	
1876	Glenorchy	
1877	Glendaruel	
	Furnace	
	Cowal	

Sources: *Oban Times, Argyllshire Herald, Argyllshire Standard, Campbeltown Courier*

Table 6   First newspaper reports of Friendly societies in Argyll
             (Ancient Order of Foresters, Loyal Order of Ancient Shepherds,
             Independent Order of Rechabites)

	AO Foresters	LOA Shepherds	IO Rechabites
1864	Easdale		
1874	Campbeltown		
1876	Ballachulish		
	Oban		
	Lochgilphead		
1878	Bonaw		
1879	Inveraray		
	Ardrishaig		
1880	Taynuilt	Lochgilphead	
1882	Tarbert		
1884		Inveraray	
1886			Oban
1887		Glencoe	Bonawe
1888		Tighnabruaich	
1889		Millhouse nr T.	
1893			Minard*
			Furnace
			Connel Ferry
			Inveraray
1894		Tarbert	Strachur*
		Luing	Bowmore
1895		Campbeltown	Lochgilphead
			Stralachlan*
1896			Glassary
1898		Ballachulish	

Sources: *Oban Times, Argyllshire Herald, Argyllshire Standard, Campbeltown Courier*

of Lorne clearly signal this (*Oban Times*, 1871 various), while later groups such as Bonaw's Granite Lodge and Furnace's Granite Lodge (*Oban Times*, 1874 and 1877 various) presumably reflect the interests of the local quarrymen. Again the contacts were likely to have been by sea between the industrial communities.

For friendly societies (see table 6), the pattern of diffusion is uneven and erratic, although again the links with sea communications and with industrial quarrying or gunpowder making villages can be picked up. In three instances of the foundings of tents of the Independent Order of Rechabites, the groups are named after or indicate acknowledgement to James Smellie, a woodmerchant who had been operating on estates in Cowal and Kintyre over a twenty year period. These three groups (marked * in Table 6) are geographically very close across Loch Fyne, and possibly interchanges among skilled operatives or support from the mutual employer may be the common factor here. In terms of social patterns, it is worth noting that there are no representatives among these societies of rural island communities, and Glassary near

Lochgilphead is the only rural mainland village community. Is this a cultural or an economic factor influencing participation in this new social habit of saving?

Other cultural activities

There are numerous examples in the newspaper records of the county of the popularity of mutual improvement societies, and literary and scientific societies. With the exception of Oban's Scientific and Literary Association which started about 1840, the majority date from 1867 onwards. Initially mutual improvement societies were found in the small towns — Campbeltown, Tobermory, Lochgilphead, Dunoon, Bowmore (*Oban Times, Argyllshire Herald, Argyllshire Standard, Campbeltown Courier*, various dates) — and may be interpreted as a response to an external political change, the extension of the franchise in the Second Reform Act of 1867. Literary and scientific societies or debating societies, founded in the same period, were to be found in the smaller communities of Port Ellen, Easdale and Ballachulish, the latter two noticeably heavier on the scientific topics in the syllabus, perhaps not unrelated to the technical aspects of local employment in the extractive slate industry. By the 1880s similar societies were appearing in much smaller communities, where in some cases the societies were clearly serving an educational function for ambitious young working class men, rather than the established middle class male audience of Oban in the 1840s and 1850s (*Oban Times, Argyllshire Herald, Argyllshire Standard, Campbeltown Courier*, various dates). In this instance the periphery is responding to change in a far distant centre, a political change which was to have significant effects on traditional forms of representation and governance at both national and local level (Cannadine, 1990: pp. 139–160).

In one other instance, Argyllshire may be seen as the centre from which an ethnic cultural movement spread out to the rest of Scotland. Oban's Lorn Ossianic Society, which met in Oban from 1872 to an apparently abrupt departure from the public record in 1881, was the forerunner of a number of Celtic club or society imitators (in Mull, with which steamer connections were the main island link, in Kintyre and in Tiree) in the later years of the 1870s and 1880s. Following extensive correspondence and articles in the *Oban Times* from October 1890, a national meeting was called in Oban in May 1891 regarding a Highland Eisteddfod (*Oban Times*, various dates). This resulted in the first Mod or meeting of *An Comunn Gaidhealach* (the Gaelic Association) which had as its objective the preservation and maintenance of the Gaelic culture and language first brought to Scotland by the Celts of Dalriada (Jackson, 1999a: p.27). Given the contemporary interest in all things Highland, the increasing social mobility generated by the railways, the range of publications in the popular press, and the large ex-Highland communities in urban centres of the Lowlands such as Glasgow, Greenock and Edinburgh, the diffusion of this particular cultural innovation was both rapid and widespread.

Concluding remarks

What general conclusions can be drawn from this examination of a range of sporting and cultural practices which underwent visible change in the later nineteenth century in the context of the peripheral Highland county of Argyll? It is clear that there was no one dominant cultural centre from which innovation diffused. Different activities arrived in the county through a range of locations, and while the major communications centres of Campbeltown in the south and Oban in the north do figure more prominently in the narrative, it was by no means exclusively from these centres that cultural diffusion occurred. A common factor in several instances clearly was the sea as communications highway, but the role of particular social groups as a mechanism of diffusion cannot be overlooked.

This peripheral rural county seems to offer evidence which does not fit the social downward diffusion model. For particular activities, it is clear that the active dissemination came through the fishermen and other working class communities: particularly in the diffusion and proselytisation of the temperance and friendly societies movements. Given the belated entry as compared with its popularity in other parts of the country, football benefited from the uptake among the urban working classes, and the majority of Argyll's clubs appear to have sprung up through working class contacts. It may be suggested, following Jarvie and Maguire (1994: p.201) that the spread of this sport is an indicator of resistance to the prevailing paternalistic ethos and power relations of rural communities but as the public records are clearly oriented to the county elite and the middle classes, there is insufficient historical evidence to substantiate this hypothesis.

This is not to gainsay the role of the gentry or the middle classes in supporting or sustaining innovation. While certain activities demonstrated social exclusivity (in time of origin, in membership, in location) and drew on wider social networks far outwith the county (in London and in the national Army), there appeared to have been a role still for the local lairds and gentry. Through subscriptions to support new activities such as literary societies or temperance clubs, through the giving of space for the playing of new sports such as football or golf, the land owning lairds continued their traditional paternalistic responsibilities to their employees (Jackson, 1998). This patronage did not decline towards the latter part of the century as Cannadine (1990) demonstrated was the case in the English shire counties.

It can thus be argued that the history of cultural diffusion in the county of Argyll demonstrates the difficulty of applying generalisations about complex social interactions based on models derived in very different social settings. While the geography and demography of the county are liable to interfere with a simple ripple model of diffusion (Bale, 1978), the social downward diffusion model does not explain many of the particular innovations discussed above. Given the pattern of land holding, it might be suggested that nowhere in Argyll was there sufficient critical mass of the elite living permanently to form a cohesive group to drive sporting change on a wide scale, nor did they wish to do so. There may have been some diminution in the traditional activities which the lairds supported, but the initiative in diffusing working class sport, especially football, and in self help societies, was apparently from the lower classes themselves. The complexity of the patterns of diffusion, which are not consistent across any of the areas of leisure activity considered, and the unevenness of development and change, suggest that particular rather than general factors must be considered in any explanation of cultural diffusion. The peripheral situation of Argyll, the underdeveloped and traditional nature of its economic base, and its cultural distinctiveness all contribute to its dissimilarity from the urban industrial society at the centre of late Victorian Britain.

References

Bailey, P. (1989) 'Leisure. culture and the historian: Reviewing the first generation of leisure historiography in Britain', *Leisure Studies* Vol. 8, No. 1: pp 107–127.

Bailey, P. (1978) *Leisure and class in Victorian England*. London: Routledge and Kegan Paul.

Bale, J. (1994) *Landscapes of modern sport*. Leicester: Leicester University Press.

———— (1978) 'Geographical diffusion and the adoption of professionalism in football in England and Wales', *Geography* Vol. 63, No. 3: pp 188–197.

Cannadine, D. (1990) *The decline and fall of the British aristocracy*. London: Yale University Press.

Clarke, J. and Critcher, C. (1985) *The devil makes work. Leisure in capitalist Britain*. London: Macmillan.

Cunningham, H. (1980) *Leisure in the industrial revolution*. London: Croom Helm.

Dunning, E. and Sheard, K. (1979) *Barbarians, gentlemen and players*. Oxford: Oxford University Press.

Ferguson, W. (1978) *Scotland: 1869 to the present*. Edinburgh: Oliver and Boyd.

Fraser, W. H. and Morris, R.J. (1990) *People and society in Scotland Volume II 1830–1914*. Edinburgh: John Donald.

Holt, R. (1998) 'Golf and the English suburb', *The Sports Historian* Vol. 18, No. 1: pp. 76–89.

———— (1989) *Sport and the British: A modern history*. Oxford: Oxford University Press.

Jackson, L. (1999a) 'Sport and Scottish Gaeldom in Argyllshire 1790–1900' in G. Jarvie (ed) *Sport in the making of Celtic cultures*. London: Leicester University Press, pp. 26–40.

———— (1999b) 'Patriotism or pleasure? The nineteenth century Volunteer force as a vehicle for rural working class male sport', *The Sports Historian* Vol. 19, No. 1: pp. 125–139.

———— (1998) 'Sport and patronage: Evidence from nineteenth century Argyllshire', *The Sports Historian* Vol. 18, No. 2: pp. 95–106.

Jarvie, G., Jackson, L. and Higgins, P. (1997) 'Scottish affairs, sporting estates and the aristocracy', *Scottish Affairs* No. 19: pp. 121–140.

Jarvie, G. and Maguire J. (1994) *Sport and leisure in social thought*. London: Routledge

Lowerson, J. (1994) 'Golf and the making of myths', in G. Jarvie and G. Walker (eds) *Scottish sport and the making of the nation*. London: Leicester University Press, pp. 75–90.

Lynch, M. (1991) *Scotland: A new history*. London: Century.

Maclagan, R.C. (1901) *The games and diversions of Argyleshire*. London: Folklore Society.

Mangan, J.A. (1983) 'Grammar schools and the games ethic in Victorian and Edwardian eras', *Albion* No. 15: pp. 313–335.

Mason, T. (ed) (1988) *Sport in Britain: A social history*. Cambridge: Cambridge University Press.

McDiarmid, D. (1976) 1876–1976. *100 years of golf at Machrihanish*. Campbeltown: *Campbeltown Courier*.

Price, R. (1989) *Scotland's golf courses*. Aberdeen: Aberdeen University Press.

Tranter, N. (1998) *Sport, economy and society in Britain 1750–1914*. Cambridge: Cambridge University Press.

———— (1989) 'Sport and the economy in nineteenth and early twentieth century Scotland', *Scottish Historical Review* Vol. LXVIII: 1, No. 185: pp. 53–69.

Vamplew, W. (1988) 'Sport and industrialisation: an economic interpretation of the change in popular sport in nineteenth century England', in J. Mangan (ed) *Pleasure, profit and proselytism. British culture and sport at home and abroad 1700–1914*. London: Frank Cass.

Walvin, J. (1978) *Leisure and society 1830–1950*. London: Longman.

Newspapers:
Argyllshire Herald, passim
Argyllshire Standard, passim
Campbeltown Courier, passim
Oban Times, passim

Selling the Arts: Centre-Periphery Tensions in Commodification Processes

Clive Gray

Department of Public Policy, De Montfort University

Introduction

The last 20 years have seen a significant number of changes occurring in the system for managing the involvement of the state in the field of arts policy. The result of these has been to mark an important move towards the commodification of this policy area, even if this process is far from complete (Gray, 2000). The purpose of this paper is to identify the political difficulties that are associated with commodifying tendencies, and the territorial implications that arise from attempts to restructure state interventions within policy areas. To this extent, at least, the focus is on the practical consequences for state actors and organisations as they attempt to come to terms with the new policy environment that is generated as a result of the move towards a more commodified form of policy structure.

Commodification and the Arts

Along with every other part of the public sector in Britain the arts have been greatly affected by the wave of reforms that have been introduced by successive governments since the early 1960s. The change of emphasis since 1979 in the reforming strategies that national Governments have pursued — towards one of attempting to create a more commodified form of public sector — has equally affected the arts, giving rise to large-scale changes in both the structures and processes that are utilised in the support and direct provision of these services. While the full extent to which the arts can be seen to have been effectively commodified in content is open to question, there is little doubt that the basic nature of the management and organisation of this policy area has been amended to display clear indications of commodifying tendencies.

The manner in which these tendencies can be seen to have been implanted within the arts policy sector has varied in terms of which area of organisational life is examined. For practical purposes commodification needs to be implemented across a number of dimensions of both organisational structure and organisational process. If any of these dimensions is not affected then commodification will not prove to be successful, even though if they are all modified there is still no guarantee that the process of change will prove successful anyway (Gray, 2000, ch. 2). The dimensions of change that need to be considered are:

- Organisational change — both in terms of the creation, abolition and reform of discrete organisations, and in terms of the internal structuring of these;
- Financial change — affecting the methods and forms of allocating financial resources to organisations;
- Managerial change — affecting the internal dynamics of organisational activity and relationships with other organisational actors; and,
- Ideological change — instilling new conceptions of the purpose of the organisation concerned and new approaches to its operations in an attempt to re-make the cultural setting within which the organisation is operating.

These forms of change are driven by the choices that are made by political actors within the system and essentially take the form of a process of trial and error: reforms are instituted and are then subject to a continuous process of modification and change in an attempt to reach some form of organisational stasis or equilibrium. The precise nature of the changes that are instituted will be primarily driven by the ideological perceptions of political actors as to the nature of the problems that require solution and what forms of solution are appropriate to the task in hand. These perceptions will be influenced by the power and other resources that are available to the actors involved which will influence, in turn, what are seen to be the potential practicalities of change.

To this extent commodification is part of a learning process on the behalf of political actors. While ideological perceptions set the framework within which change is managed the practical consequences of organisational reform — in the form of both intended and unintended consequences, and as a result of the inter-organisational political oppositions that will be created — generate further considerations that require resolution. The result of this is that organisational change is an ongoing process that must be expected to generate new patterns of political activity both within and between sets of organisational actors (Pollitt, 1984, ch. 11; Rhodes, 1997; Stoker, 1999).

In this respect the arts are no different to other policy sectors within British government. The processes of commodification have seen the development of new styles of political activity within this sector that have been intended to create new patterns of service delivery with the overall intention of remaking the nature of arts policy itself. While commodification has not yet advanced to the stage where the arts are completely treated as any other consumer good that is available in the open market, the clear drive of policy towards this end is well advanced. This process, however, has not been a simple one whereby the wishes of central political actors have been simply imposed on a malleable system. Instead the range of already existing participants have acted as classic intervening variables, serving to modify and adapt central wishes in terms of their own perspectives.

The extent to which actors other than those in the central positions of power and authority within the political system are capable of using their location within policy networks to undertake this manipulative strategy has important implications, not only for the commodification process itself but also for an understanding of the importance of locational factors in influencing the processes of organisational and policy reform. Given that the arts policy sector is geographically divided between multiple actors at the national, regional and local levels of the political system it provides an interesting case study of the mechanisms that are involved in the processes of change that have been applied in the move towards commodified policy systems.

The arts policy sector

The structure of the organisational network for managing state involvement with the arts in Britain is characterised by the seemingly contradictory features of "organisational diversity and value limitation, which lead to an institutional pluralism but a behavioural elitism" (Gray, 1993: pp. 9–10). In brief, the policy sector is characterised by the existence of a multitude of organisational actors providing varied forms of support for the arts but operating within a closely defined set of preferred options for the operation of policy. These ideological values serve to limit the autonomy of organisational actors in important ways when dealing with the arts and culture (see Street, 1997, ch. 5), and allow for the exercise of an effectively oligarchical dominance over the multiple organisations that inhabit the sector.

In addition to this structural dimension must also be added the fact that the 'arts' as a policy issue are of distinctly low political status. The traditional British reluctance to become involved in the provision, maintenance and support of the arts on the behalf of the state — exemplified by Lord Melbourne's comment in 1835, "God help the government who meddles in art" (Minihan, 1977: p. 60) — has led to marked differences between Britain and her Continental neighbours which tend to be much more interventionist in attitude. While the British state has developed a complex network of forms of support for the arts since 1945 this has been in the context of a desire to treat them as a depoliticised arena of activity.

As such it is hardly surprising that the arts in Britain have received little political engagement from core actors in Westminster and Whitehall. Instead there has been a tendency to manage the arts through 'arm's-length' organisational forms in the shape of various quangos (such as the Arts Councils (ACs) and Regional Arts Boards [RABs]), or through local authorities. This choice has the obvious advantage for central political actors of avoiding accusations of political bias or censorship in the provision of the arts, whilst also ensuring that some form of provision is undertaken. In this respect the arts form a good example of 'low politics': "residual matters" of "embellishment and detail" (Bulpitt, 1983: pp. 3, 29) that can be safely hived-off from detailed central control.

The pattern that this reluctance to become centrally involved in the management and direct provision of the arts has generated contributes to the organisational pluralism that is a central feature of this policy sector by disaggregating policy control to multiple institutional sites. It has also allowed key actors within this fragmented organisational universe the opportunity to impose their own ideologies and values upon the policy sector as a consequence of the establishment of a policy vacuum as far as the centre is concerned. The mutual reinforcement that existed between the structure of the policy sector and (a relative lack of) central state involvement with it allowed for the creation of a stable environment for arts policy until the 1980s. The first steps towards commodification arising at that time, however, served to alter the game that was being played: a more interventionist central state began to change the stability that had been created in the post-war period, leading to a restructuring of the arts network.

The extent to which the centre has been able to impose a new form of policy sector on the arts has not been a tale of simple direction. Instead, there has been a process of effective trial-and-error taking place as the multiple changes that are a necessary part of the commodification process have been worked through. The arts network has itself been a key participant in this process with local, regional and national actors all playing a part in the modification of the sector. The still unfinished business of commodifying the arts sector demonstrates the difficulties that face reforming central governments in changing long-established patterns of inter-relationships between organisational actors that are operating at a remove from the centre. How local and regional actors have affected the direction, speed and scope of commodification needs to be examined to understand what has been taking place in the arts over the last 20 years.

Locality and the commodification of the arts

The fact that the arts policy sector is made up of independent organisational actors, each operating within their own geographically de-limited areas, necessarily implies that there will be an element of autonomy in the choices that will be made by these actors in the pursuit of policy goals, whether their own or those of central government. While some actors, notably the ACs for England, Scotland and Wales, have a greater impact on the operations of the entire sector as a consequence of their greater financial resources and their support for dominant values within the system, other organisational actors cannot be discounted as being significant participants within the arts policy sector (Gray, 2000: ch. 3).

The major reason for this importance for regional and local actors lies in the weaknesses of central control over the policy sector. While the centre has become increasingly intrusive in the entire field of leisure policy since the establishment of the Department for Culture, Media and Sport (DCMS) in 1992 (Taylor, 1997) it has yet to develop a dominant policy role in the arts. The, at least, semi-independence of the key providers of state support for the arts (the ACs, RABs and local authorities) has meant that the centre has had to largely rely on methods of persuasion and encouragement to see the changes that it desires take place. Even when the centre is seemingly in a position to implement its desired options the fact that there already exist operational networks of participants within the sector serves to ensure that the process of change is a contested one, with no guarantee that the centre will get its own way. In the case of the arts this can be illustrated by the machinations surrounding the reform of the regional level of arts support in England following the publication of the Wilding Report (1989).

The establishment of a regional dimension to the arts support system was a direct response to the decision of the AC of Great Britain to close its' own regional offices in the mid-1950s. Arts activists and local authorities began a process of creating their own intermediate organisations, the Regional Arts Associations (RAAs), to fill the void that was created by this decision. The RAAs were dominated by local interests — often working to different criteria to those supported by the AC of Great Britain — with this leading to an increasing number of conflicts between the two sets of organisational actors. These conflicts were intensified under the Conservative Governments after 1979 as the economic concerns of central government permeated the entire public sector.

In effect the conflict between the RAAs and the central actors of the AC of Great Britain and central government itself was based on incompatible sets of arguments held by each of the participants. The RAAs wished to retain their local links and to increase their involvement within the system of arts funding and support; the AC of Great Britain wished to preserve its own centrality within this system and to maintain its own aesthetic and artistic principles as the dominant ones; and central government wished to strengthen economic management and accountability within the arts (Beck, 1995; Gray, 2000: ch. 6). While the final result was to see the replacement of the locally-dominated RAAs with the centrally-dominated Regional Arts Boards (RABs) the final shape of the reform process was not determined by the simple imposition of central wishes.

In part this result was the consequence of matters outside of the intrinsic merits of the respective arguments that the participants were making. The low political salience of the arts as a policy sector meant that the process of reform saw three separate Ministers involved — Richard Luce, David Mellor and Timothy Renton — each of whom took a different view of the form that change should take (implying a lack of a coherent governmental strategy in this area), and each of whom had different levels of support within central government for their activities. Equally, the RAAs had themselves developed an increasingly professionalised and bureaucratised central forum — the Council of Regional Arts Associations (CoRAA) (Evans and Taylor, 1994) — which served as an effective pressure-group during the reform process, defending the regional perspective against central arguments. These structural factors served to dilute the ability of the centre to simply impose its own will on the arts support system.

While the final result was to see the development of a centralising trend within the arts policy sector it was not as uninhibitingly centralising as it might have been. The local links of the RAAs with local communities and organisations have been weakened, but in return the RABs have been given an increased share of the overall arts budget to manage, rising from 24 per cent of AC expenditure in 1988/89 to 31 per cent in 1996/ 97 (Gray, 2000: p. 150). To some extent the compromise conclusion to the reform of the RAAs was inevitable given the differences of opinion held by the core participants in the process, particularly given the lack of political significance that the arts have as a policy sector, but the ability of regional actors to exact concessions from the centre should not be under-estimated. Developments since the establishment of the RABs have shown that the regional level is becoming an increasingly important element of the arts support system in England (DCMS, 1999a), and that their establishment has not resolved the fundamental structural problems that it was intended they should. Indeed, given the locational position of the RABs within the arts support system it is unlikely that the inter-organisational conflicts that exist could be resolved given the conflicting demands between centre and locality that they continue to embody.

A similar position can be found in the case of more local actors within the arts sector, the local authorities. Local government has always been composed of independent political systems in their own right, with the capability of making autonomous policy choices for their areas of competence. Given this policy autonomy it should be expected that there would be considerable variation between local authorities in terms of their arts policies, just as there is in every other policy area that they are concerned with (Wilson and Game, 1998: pp. 118–9). This expectation is reinforced by the fact that the arts (and cultural policy issues in general) are only discretionary areas of activity for local authorities in England and Wales, unlike the statutory requirements of, for example, education, housing and social services. The discretionary nature of arts provision in local government in England and Wales requires, therefore, a degree of political commitment on the behalf of councillors and officers that is not present with statutory services, which have to be provided, regardless of such commitment.

The consequence of this is that there are distinct variations in support for the arts between local authorities: Williams *et al.* (1995), for example, showed that three times as many urban authorities had specific arts officers in place compared with rural authorities, and that 76 per cent of urban authorities spent over £2.50 per capita on the arts compared with only 9 per cent of rural authorities. The extent to which such differences are directly attributable to variations in commitment, and how much to the disparity of resources between urban and rural authorities is debatable. American evidence implies that there are 'economies of agglomeration' in the performing arts, with urbanisation generating concentrations of artistic output (Heilbrun and Gray, 1993: p. 304), implying that local authorities are simply responding to their local populations in an unmediated fashion. Decisions on staffing and expenditure, however, depend upon the exercise of political choice, implying that local circumstances must be interpreted and acted upon in a conscious fashion, thus implying that a commitment to the arts within local government needs to be considered in more detail.

The changing pattern of local authority involvement in the arts would certainly provide support for the idea that local political choice is a key element in their management and provision at a local level. Certainly specific decisions about the provision of resources for the performing arts are heavily influenced by the precise circumstances that local councillors, in particular, are faced by (Street, 1995). More general matters, such as the management of commodifying tendencies, however, are usually less place specific and are more ideologically determined, implying that local effects need to be understood in this context rather than any other in the first instance.

The problems confronting the centre when attempting to undertake structural reforms at the regional level in the arts sector have been, in many cases, multiplied in the case of the local level. This has been primarily a consequence of the multiple forms of change that have been involved in the movement towards a more commodified status for the arts. By requiring change to take place across a number of dimensions of the arts support system governments, both local and central, are confronted by the need to construct a number of different strategies for successful implementation. As this increases the number of decision points that are involved in the process of change it is not surprising to see that a relatively simple process (as far as the centre is concerned anyway) becomes a much more politically-charged and contentious set of issue areas.

This political complication is increased by the fact that, regardless of the centralising trends affecting local government over the last 20 years (Wilson and Game, 1998), local authorities still retain the power of independent choice. To this extent, if no other, the differences between local authorities in terms of what they wish to achieve in the field of the arts, and how the arts are perceived within local government, are both important factors to consider. In this respect the changes that have been taking place in local government towards a more commodified conception of the role of the arts in local areas has clearly influenced the policy initiatives that have been developed in recent years as a response to this.

Perhaps the most important of these new initiatives has been the linkage of the arts with issues of local economic development at an increasing rate since the early 1980s. This development had two clear precursors in the activities of the Greater London Council (GLC) in the 1980s and the publication of Myerscough's (1988) *The Economic Importance of the Arts*. The former of these was important in that they were predicated upon a view of the arts as having an explicit political dimension to them which went against the dominant aesthetic and artistic values that were held within the national arts oligopoly, represented at that time by the AC of Great Britain and the Office of Arts and Libraries in central government. In this view the arts could be used to empower disadvantaged groups within society by providing them with their own voice through the use of broader cultural and artistic tools than were then available. This empowerment strategy was supported by a shift in power and resources towards community-based groups and a move away from the 'high' arts towards more 'popular' forms of expression, such as photography, popular music and video (Gray, 2000: pp. 164-5).

The GLC was also important in developing the move towards treating the arts as a tool for local economic development (GLC, 1985). This move was still, however, predicated upon fairly traditional ideas about the role of the state in such issues and certainly did not incorporate the assumptions about the 'superiority' of the market over political forms of resource allocation that are a common feature of the commodification process. Even without such preconceptions, however, the arts were still placed in a secondary position in the economic development process. The emphasis was definitely placed on the arts as a sector of economic production, distribution and exchange rather than on them as a source of use-value in their own right. The idea that the arts sector could be managed as simply another set of economic resources was boosted by an acceptance that it was a contributor to local economies, not only through the employment and expenditure that it generated itself, but also through its role in encouraging spill-over effects into other forms of economic activity (such as tourism).

The situation of the arts in local government changed rapidly as it became increasingly argued that the arts were not simply capable of producing aesthetic pleasures but were also important components of a new political economy: creating "a climate of optimism ... developing the 'can do' culture" (Arts Council of Great Britain, 1988: p. 2) that the Conservative governments of the 1980s and 1990s supported. The consequence of this was that the arts became increasingly associated with other areas of local authority work — particularly planning and economic development. The results of this depended upon which local authority is examined: in some cases it was no more than using the arts as a promotional tool to stimulate tourism (Williams et al, 1995), in others they were utilised as a direct tool for economic development, even if the evidence to demonstrate the effectiveness of using the arts in this way was, at best, ambiguous (Griffiths, 1993).

The new importance that was attached to the arts as a consequence of using them as part of a broader approach to the fulfilment of other policy objectives demonstrated both the policy weaknesses of the arts as an independent sector, and the increased emphasis on economic criteria as the estimation of policy worth that is a part and parcel of commodification. Between them these created a climate that was driven, not by the requirements of the arts themselves but, instead, by alternative estimations of policy worth that did not share the dominant values of the various oligarchies within the arts network. The precise pattern of involvement of the arts with these alternative views had, of course, to be determined by the relevant policy actors within each local authority, and how they understood the role of the arts.

The consequence of this was that there has been a proliferation of new developments affecting the arts across Britain, from the development of 'cultural quarters' (as, for example, in Sheffield and Huddersfield), to major infrastructural and educational investment in the arts (as, for example, in Birmingham). Such developments, however, are extremely localised ones: there is still no effective regional or national policy to lead the process of change. Local authorities have had to react autonomously to take on board both the range of general pressures that have been placed upon them by central governments (from Compulsory Competitive Tendering to Best Value), and the new opportunities that face the arts through their increasingly recognised policy importance. As such it is hardly surprising that there has been no single path to the development of a commodified policy system for the arts.

While central government has recently begun the process of attempting to encourage a more co-ordinated approach to the development of regional and local strategies for the arts and cultural policies in England (Department of Culture, Media and Sport, 1999a, 1999b) these depend upon the willingness of local and regional actors to create them. In Scotland, however, there is now a statutory duty on local authorities to make provision for the arts with the new Scottish Parliament having overall responsibility for this policy area. Overall, however, there is still an absence of anything approaching a co-ordinated policy towards the arts for Britain meaning that the choices of local and regional actors are still of key importance in this policy area. Given this it must be expected that diversity and difference will continue to be the order of the day for the foreseeable future.

Conclusion

It cannot be doubted that the process of commodification has had a major impact upon the arts within Britain (Gray, 2000). However, this development has been locationally specific, depending upon the precise circumstances that have faced individual areas and actors. The weaknesses of the arts as a policy area have contributed to the partial nature of the developments that have been taking place, leading to a situation where the interpretation of the requirements of what is required for the arts has been left to the willingness and ability of local actors to determine. These actors have therefore been able to exercise autonomy over the processes of commodification, leading to differences between localities in terms of the specific nature of the managerial and ideological changes that have taken place as part of these processes of change.

Where local actors have been weakest in exercising autonomy has been in the organisational and financial areas of change, where the choices and decisions of national actors have been more significant in affecting what takes place locally. Even here, however, as the example of the development of the RABs showed, local and regional actors have been able to affect the specific nature of the changes that have been taking place, implying that the processes of commodification are not subject to simple imposition from the centre. The ability of local and regional actors to intervene in the process of commodification indicates that this is a process that is a politically contested area of activity that cannot be seen as a top-down process alone, but must also take on board the specifics of locality as well.

Commodification may be a process that is dependent, in the first instance at least, upon the choices and decisions of national political actors who set the parameters within which reform takes place. These boundaries around change, however, are then subject to interpretation at the regional and local levels, leading to variations in both the speed and direction that it takes. If the locational specificity of change is not taken into account then any analysis of the processes involved in the re-creation of policy arenas to match nationally-determined choices must be partial in nature.

References

Arts Council of Great Britain (1988) *An urban renaissance*. London: Arts Council of Great Britain.

Beck, A. (1995) *The Wilding review*. Paper to Cultural Policy and Politics Research Group, Liverpool University.

Bulpitt, J. (1983) *Territory and power in the United Kingdom*. Manchester: Manchester University Press.

Department for Culture, Media and Sport (1999a) *Regional cultural consortiums*. London: Department of Culture, Media and Sport.

——— (1999b) *Local cultural strategies*. London: Department of Culture, Media and Sport.

Evans, B. and A. Taylor (1994) 'The rise of the intermediate level institution in British public administration', *Public Administration* Vol. 72: pp. 551–72.

Gray, C. (1993) *The network for cultural policy in Britain*. Paper to Political Studies Association Annual Conference, University of Leicester.

——— (2000) *The politics of the arts in Britain*. London: Macmillan.

Greater London Council (1985) *The state of the art*. London: Greater London Council.

Griffiths, R. (1993) 'The politics of cultural policy in urban regeneration strategies', *Policy and Politics*, Vol. 21: pp. 39–46.

Heilbrun, J. and C. M. Gray (1993) *The economics of art and culture*. Cambridge, Cambridge University Press.

Minihan, J. (1977) *The nationalization of culture*. London, Hamish Hamilton.

Myerscough, J. (1988) *The economic importance of the arts*. London: Policy Studies Institute.

Pollitt, C. (1984) *Manipulating the machine*. London: Allen and Unwin.

Rhodes, R. (1997) *Understanding governance*. Buckingham: Open University Press.

Stoker, G. (1999) 'Introduction: The unintended costs and benefits of new management reform for British local government', in G. Stoker (ed) *The new management of British local governance*. London: Macmillan, pp. 1–21.

Street, J. (1995) 'Making fun: The local politics of popular music', in J. Lovenduski and J. Stanyer (eds) *Contemporary political studies 1995*. Belfast, Political Studies Association of the United Kingdom, pp. 316–23.

——— (1997) *Politics and popular culture*. Cambridge: Polity Press.

Taylor, A. (1997) '"Arm's length but hands on": mapping the new governance', *Public Administration* Vol. 75: pp. 441–66.

Wilding Report (1989) *Supporting the arts: a review of the structure of arts funding*. London: Office of Arts and Libraries.

Williams, A., Shaw, G. and Huber, M. (1995) 'The arts and economic development', *Regional Studies* Vol. 29: pp. 73–80.

Wilson, D. and C. Game (1998) *Local government in the United Kingdom* (2nd Edition). London: Macmillan.

Technological Development and Changing Leisure Practices

Jo Bryce

Department of Psychology
University of Central Lancashire

Introduction and background

It is widely claimed that developments in information and communication tecnologies (ICTs) and the increasing use of the Internet have important consequences for business, work, education, and society as a whole. There is an increasingly large literature examining the relationship between technological change, the Internet and aspects of contemporary society. One aspect of this relationship that has not been sufficiently addressed in either the technology or leisure literature is the relationship between technology and leisure. The ESRC's Virtual Society? Program[1] funded 22 projects investigating the impact of ICTs and Internet use on contemporary society. Interestingly, none of these projects specifically addressed the issue of how technological developments such as the Internet may be related to changing leisure practices. This is surprising considering the size of the computer gaming industry and other leisure-based technologies. For example, the leisure software industry is estimated as being worth $5.5 billion in Europe, with $3.5 billion of that being in the UK (ELSPA, 2000). The importance of computer and Internet use as a leisure activity is also suggested by recent US research which found that one third of 4,000 surveyed Internet users engaged in entertainment activities via this medium (Nie and Erbring, 2000). The size of the market, and the number of people using the Internet and computer gaming technologies during their leisure time, highlight the need to investigate the economic, social and psychological aspects of leisure-related computer use. It has been claimed that the use of computer technology, particularly that used for computer gaming, lags behind the theory of ICT use in work and education (Yates and Littleton, 1998). The aim of this paper is to demonstrate the need to investigate the relationship between technology and leisure from a perspective that is informed by wider debates in the literature on technology and society, as well as themes and debates in the leisure literature.

The media, industry and academic discourses surrounding developments in ICTs, and their influence on contemporary society has been criticized for treating the emergence of ICTs and the Internet as a revolutionary event. Theorists such as Winston (1998) claim that events hyperbolized as a technological revolution can be more usefully viewed as a more evolutionary and less transformative process. Winston shows how previous technological developments, such as the invention of the telegraph and radio, rather than emerging suddenly as the results of a leap of innovation, evolved slowly over a number of years through the work of a number of scientists and inventors. As with previous technological developments, the Internet has evolved rather than suddenly emerging to transform everyday life. A discussion of the historical development of the Internet is beyond the scope of the current paper, but accounts of the development of this technology can be found in Castells (2000) and Slevin (2000).

Historically, the emergence of new technologies (e.g., radio and the telegraph) has always been accompanied by debates regarding the positive or negative influences of such developments for society (Winston, 1998). The polarization of discourses between utopian or dystopian futures engendered by technological development is common during periods of technological change (op. cit.):

> Does it not mean the breaking down of artificial national barriers and the welding of humanity into one composite whole? Does it not mean that each is given a chance to comprehend the significance of national and international affairs, and that all the evils of jealousy and hatred being thus displayed before the world will be no longer fester, but be cleansed by the antiseptic of common understanding and common sense? (Lewis 1924: p. 144, quoted by Woolgar, 2000)

This quotation demonstrates the extreme nature of predictions made in light of technological development, and is consistent with media and academic discourses examining the influence of ICTs and the Internet on contemporary society. However, polarization of opinion around utopian or dystopian technological futures has been criticized for taking an overly simplistic and uniform approach to the effects of new technologies (Slevin, 2000). Media, government and academic debates center alternatively around the utopian view that ICTs and the Internet provide unprecedented opportunities for freedom of information, empowerment, democracy and social inclusion. The contradictory or dystopian view portrays the Internet as dangerous, encouraging deviance, anarchy and increasing social isolation, loss of community and depression. Rather than pursue such polarized discourses, it has been recently claimed that an investigation of the multiple uses of the Internet and ICTs is required, highlighting the benefits of recognizing the communicative potentialities of the technology, rather than viewing its effects as uniformly good or bad for society (Slevin, 2000). This is consistent with the need to study the everyday uses of ICTs and the Internet, the meanings attached to it by users (Hine, 2000), and the diversity of leisure practices supported by these emerging technologies.

Technology and leisure: historical and contemporary perspectives

The relationship between technology and leisure activities and experiences is not new. Historically, technological developments such as radio, cinema and public transport have all been related to changing leisure organization and experience (see Argyle, 1996; Bryce, 2001; Rojek, 2000). Such technologies have formed, and continue to form, an important part of contemporary leisure practice. Alongside these existing leisure technologies, personal computers, gaming consoles and the Internet have emerged as significant locations of leisure activity in contemporary society.

The relationship between technological development and changing leisure practices is linked to the communicative potentialities of new technologies. Such developments have made it possible "to revise ordinary orientations of leisure by dramatically increasing our sense of interdependence and our access to information and entertainment" (Rojek, 2000: p. 24). Leisure-related use of the Internet is closely linked to increased opportunities for communication and organization which allow the formation of virtual communities. Many of these communities are organized around leisure lifestyles or ideologies within which the exchange of information, social support and the formation of social networks are central aspects of the leisure experience. It is this potential which supports a variety of internet uses on a continuum from 'socially acceptable' to 'antisocial' or 'deviant'. The development of virtual communities needs to be investigated in the particular rather than viewing the emergence of these social groups as having overall positive or negative implications for society and individual well-being (Hine, 2000).

Although many of the major themes in the leisure literature have relevance to the relationship between technological development and changing leisure practices, it is beyond the scope of this paper to give detailed coverage of all of these themes. In the following section, themes such as leisure meaning and function, the temporal and spatial organization of leisure, and access and inclusion are discussed in relation to leisure-related Internet use. Discussion of these themes is pursued in an attempt to open an informative dialogue between leisure theorists and those studying the influence of ICTs on contemporary society, and highlight areas for future research.

Leisure meaning and function

The meanings and functions attached to leisure practices by individuals are well established in the literature. Leisure has been identified as meeting a number of different needs and functions; for example, relaxation, stimulation, escape, social interaction, the development of self-identity and lifestyle (Kabanoff, 1982). Despite the lack of research addressing the issue of the meaning and function of leisure in relation to technology, it seems likely that ICTs and Internet use fulfill the same functions as other leisure activities and practices (Bryce, 2001). In particular, it seems likely that realization of the communicative potential of the Internet to support the social and affiliative functions of leisure is a particularly important motivation for Internet use. This continuity of leisure functions and motivations suggests an associated continuity of meanings attached to activities performed or participated through technological media. Despite this, there is a need for research which addresses these issues in more detail and examines how leisure practices and activities may create an impetus for technological innovation.

Classifications of technological leisure

Classifications of leisure activities and their consequences for psychological well-being are central to leisure research. The serious/casual leisure dichotomy (Stebbins, 1982, 1997) is of particular relevance to the investigation of the relationship between technology and leisure (Bryce, 2001). Where computer gaming and Internet use have been considered in the literature, they have been considered as casual, to a large extent passive, and potentially detrimental to mental and physical health (Griffiths, 1997; Bryce, 2001). However, the multiplicity of uses of the Internet and computer technology makes such classifications difficult. Internet use and computer gaming may be considered serious leisure pursuits by some individuals, or they may encompass the subtypes of casual leisure (Stebbins, 1997; Bryce, 2001). Computer use cannot be regarded solely as passive entertainment, as the variety of activities supported by this technology exhibit varying levels of skill, activity, knowledge and experience. Again, this demonstrates the need for research which recognizes the ability of the Internet and computer use to support a variety of different leisure practices, rather than viewing the potentialities of these technologies as static and uniform.

Spatial and temporal organization of leisure

Another important issue to be considered is the extent to which new communication technologies are changing the spatial and temporal organization of society, and the implications of this for the organization and experience of leisure. The domestic, work-related, educational and leisure-related aspects of Internet use illustrate the intersection of traditional and virtual leisure spaces and changing work-home/work-leisure distinctions (Bryce, 2001). The increasing commercialization of the Internet and on-line leisure practices such as shopping also suggest a blurring of domestic and commercial leisure spaces. Contemporary leisure spaces, then, may be experienced as multiple, diverse, and simultaneous (Bryce, 2001). Such spaces have been described as analogous to Foucault's concept of "heterotopic space" (Foucault, 1986: p. 25). It has been claimed that such spaces exist independently of technological phenomena such as the Internet, in urban leisure spaces such as shopping malls and airports (Bryce, 2001; Rojek, 1995). These 'disembedded leisure spaces' are already integral to contemporary leisure experiences, but the anonymity and disinhibiting potentials of the Internet create leisure spaces in which the merging in one space of fact, fantasy and reality are particularly apparent (Bryce, 2001; Rojek, 2000).

It has also been claimed that, in cyberspace, reality is detached from its temporal and spatial orderings (Castells, 2000). Home computing and the Internet challenge traditional conceptions of the spatial and interactional organization of leisure by blurring the boundaries between domestic, virtual and commercial leisure spaces (Bryce, 2001). Individuals are able to engage simultaneously in synchronous and asynchronous communication from geographically diverse locations during their leisure time. In 'Multi User Dungeons' (MUDs) and online computer gaming, individuals may experience temporal and spatial arrangements differently; sense of time and place may change in ways consistent with the flow or optimal experience framework (Csikszentmihalyi, 1975; see Bryce and Higgins, 2000 for a discussion of the use of this framework to investigate the phenomenology of computer use). Conversely, in other online activities supporting leisure practices, such as fan cultures etc., online interaction may also be, to a certain extent, determined by events off-line. This suggests that in certain groups or activities there are changes in the spatial and temporal aspects of leisure practices. However, such changes must be investigated from the perspective of the user to examine how they experience the various arrangements of temporality and spatiality in online interactions, and how online leisure practices are constructed in relation to the temporal and spatial organization of leisure practices offline (Hine, 2000). The temporal and spatial arrangements of virtual leisure spaces are constructed around the social practices of individuals and groups (Hine, 2000), and the meanings they attach to these practices. The identification of the processes through which virtual leisure spaces are constructed and imbued with symbolic meaning is an important area for further research, requiring a recognition of the diversity of the activities and practices supported by new leisure technologies.

Virtual communities as leisure spaces

The Internet supports a multiplicity of leisure spaces and activities, but how should the notion of virtual leisure spaces be conceptualized? There is a large body of research which investigates the organization and authenticity of virtual communities. Virtual communities have been defined as the "Social aggregations that emerge from the Net when enough people carry on those public discussions long enough, with sufficient human feelings, to form webs of personal relationships" (Rheingold, 1993: p. 5). These social aggregations are the location of leisure practices and activities which form a significant amount of leisure activity for a number of people. The concept of virtual community covers a wide variety of social spaces and groups in cyberspace. Newsgroups, MUDs, IRCs (Internet Relay Chat) are organized around different topics, and have different rationales and functions for their creation. The various functions of these groups include the provision of social support, coverage of media issues, social action, friendships and dating, fan cultures, and online gaming (Bryce, 2001; Wellman and Gullia, 1999).

Virtual communities also support more extreme ideologies or deviant activities such as race hate, sexual interest in children and hacking. This demonstrates the continuum which exists in the nature and social acceptability of virtual communities. Many of these spaces are socially constructed around leisure ideologies, interests and lifestyles, emphasizing the claim that "cyberspace is predicated on knowledge and information" (Jones, 1999: p. 15). This suggests that people organize globally around specific political ideologies, leisure lifestyles and practices, so that in cyberspace 'ideography replaces geography' (Holderness, 1994a). However, it is likely that the extent to which communities are comprised of a diversity of geographically located individuals depends on the specificity of the ideography, and the extent to which this ideology is viewed as socially acceptable or deviant. Virtual communities based around socially acceptable leisure lifestyles such as football, fan culture and computer gaming may be more strongly geographically bound than those based around extreme or deviant leisure practices. For example, in communities based around deviant or illegal interests such as sexual interest in children, the identification or availability of individuals sharing a similar ideography in local contexts may be problematic and/or place the individual at risk from prosecution.

There are varying opinions in the literature regarding the authenticity of virtual communities. Utopian visions view virtual communities as a new public realm where humanity can recreate the sense of community lost in off-line society (Rheingold, 1993; Jones, 1995; Schuler, 1996). In particular, the social and informational resources available in certain types of virtual communities, particularly in self-help groups, may fulfill an important function in improving physical and mental health (Wellman and Gullia, 1999). The anonymity of cyberspace may actually encourage the active seeking of help and information by individuals who may feel unable to seek help in offline settings.

Other theorists have questioned the authenticity of virtual communities and their ability to be experienced in the same ways as their offline equivalent (Kling, 1996; Doheny-Fanna, 1996). Debates concerning the nature of community in wider socio-logical and cultural literature is beyond the scope of the current paper but such debates feature in the discussions of the authenticity of virtual communities and their relation to off-line community (see Jones, 1998). Criticisms of virtual communities focus on claims that the narrowband of information exchanged and the specificity of interests and lifestyles around which virtual communities form takes a narrow understanding of community (Kling, 1996). Similarly, Doheny-Fanna (1996) claims that due to the anonymity and lower levels of commitment and loyalty required in virtual communities, membership of these social groups may be temporary and less fulfilling than real community membership.

The polarization within the literature on the authenticity of virtual communities fails to recognize the diversity of functions and organization of these groups. The meanings attached to membership of virtual communities will differ according to their structure and function. For example, gaming communities will differ in certain respects to those of self-help groups for suffers of depression or survivors of child sexual abuse. Authenticity of these communities and the informational or social support they provide cannot be judged without investigating community members' understanding and experiences of involvement in their particular community (Hine, 2000). Further research is required to look at the leisure-related aspects of virtual community development and membership that recognizes the multiplicity of organizing ideologies of different communities. Such research requires consideration of how individuals construct their experiences and meanings attached to community membership. Methods such as online or virtual ethnography (in which the researcher, to a greater or lesser extent, becomes a member of that community and achieves an insider's perspective of the community: see Hine, 2000) are most suitable for such research.

Research is also required to look at the intersection of individuals' membership of online and offline communities. Individuals are simultaneously members of a multiplicity of communities (Etzioni, 1995). Rather than seeing these as separate entities, there is a need to examine the ways in which on-line and off-line community membership overlap and may be mutually influential (Kendall, 1997). Aspects of offline contexts enable and constrain online participation — e.g. workplace, leisure time, domestic responsibilities and income (Kendall, 1997) — in similar ways to the concept of leisure constraints (Crawford *et al.*, 1991). The intersection of offline and online events illustrates the ability of the Internet and ICTs to blur accepted boundaries between different areas of human existence: between work and leisure, fantasy and reality, and domestic and commercial leisure spaces.

The domestic and the commercial: consumer e-commerce

Developments in ICTs and the Internet are also blurring the divisions between domestic and commercial spaces. Consumer e-commerce and on-line shopping are changing spatial and temporal dimensions of consumption. E-commerce is defined as "the purchase of goods, services and other financial transactions in which the interactive process is mediated by information or digital technology at both, locationally separate, ends of the interchange" (The Retail E-commerce Task Force, 2000). Online shopping allows immediate checking of stock availability and ordering without the time restrictions of offline retail. Research suggests that the most frequently purchased goods in online transactions are computer software, travel tickets, books and CDs (Rutter and Southerton, 2000). Retailers and businesses are currently heralding consumer e-commerce and online shopping as the future of retailing, although research shows that issues of trust and security in online interactions are significant barriers to the uptake of consumer e-commerce (Rutter and Southerton, 2000). Other barriers to the spread of consumer e-commerce are socioeconomic factors such as income and class, which affect access to technology and the ability to purchase goods online (Rutter and Southerton, 2000). The experience of purchasing goods offline and its translation into digital forms of consumption suggests that consumer e-commerce may not become the all-encompassing shopping revolution claimed by its proponents. For example, the purchasing of clothes online is less popular and this has been explained in terms of the inability to translate the social and leisure-related aspects of consumption into online contexts (Rutter and Southerton, 2000). Shopping is an enjoyable leisure activity for many people, one that often involves social interaction and companionship, the experiencing of browsing, and does not solely involve the purchase of goods. The convenience of purchasing online may make certain types of goods suitable for consumer e-commerce, but the experience of consumption is not related solely to purchasing. It is also located in social and leisure practices that require further consideration by academics, government and business.

Constraint: access and inclusion in the information society

Freedom, choice and access are central to the concept of leisure (Neulinger, 1974) but certain factors, such as income, gender and race, may limit access to leisure activities and spaces (Crawford and Jackson, 1991). Research investigating the experience of leisure constraints and the mechanisms by which individuals negotiate or resist such constraints are an important theme in the leisure literature. These constraints are also relevant to a discussion of leisure practices surrounding the Internet, as gender, race and income are frequently discussed as barriers to access and participation online (see later section). The identification of these constraining factors and government efforts to develop ways of overcoming them is apparent in government and academic discourses about social inclusion, both with regard to leisure participation in general, and in relation to new technology. From both the technology and leisure literature, two classes of constraint relevant to the use of new technologies for leisure are identified.

Access constraints

Income is potentially the most important determinant of Internet access; a new computer with modem costs approximately one years unemployment benefit in the UK (Holderness, 1994a). The ability to afford and maintain the technology which provides Internet access demonstrates that claims for the empowering nature of the Internet is only available to those who can afford access (Bryce, 2001). It has been estimated that only 14 % of the population have access to the Internet in UK, (Hine, 2000), and issues of access to technology based on income and class have been cited in the literature examining the uptake of consumer e-commerce. For example, it has been claimed that e-commerce favours the professional and middle classes who have the resources to participate in consumer e-commerce and are not subject to the same financial constraints as working class or the unemployed. Class A, B and C1 have greater access to PCs, they make up 77% of UK Internet users but only 57% of the UK population (Rutter and Southerton, 2000). Lansbury (2000) provides figures to suggest that approximately two thirds of British households headed by a professional have a PC, four times greater than households headed by unskilled or manual workers, and that lower income households are less likely to be Internet users. Such figures demonstrate that lower income families and individuals are more likely to be excluded from on-line leisure practices, as well as being constrained in everyday leisure participation. From this perspective, existing constraints and barriers to leisure participation are reinforced by technological developments. The lower uptake of Internet use in lower income groups may also be related to the technological literacy needed to use the Internet (see next section).

Participation constraints

The second class of constraints to leisure-related Internet use are those which influence the ability of individuals to participate fully in online interactions. It has been claimed in utopian discourses surrounding the Internet that constraints to participation such as race and gender are overcome by the anonymity of online interaction (Smith and Kollock, 1999). This, it has been claimed, provides the opportunity for individuals to create their own identity, and to be accepted for their conduct and communications, rather than by social markers such as gender, class, race etc. (Smith and Kollock, 1999). However, there is much evidence to suggest that the constraining influence of gender and race continue to be influential in online interactions (see Burkhalter, 1999 and O'Brien, 1999 for a discussion of the persistence of race and gender in online inter-action). Research on Internet users suggests that the majority of Internet users are white middle class males and/or academics and professionals. There are a variety of estimates of women's Internet use but they are believed to represent between 31-45% of Internet users (Kendal, 1999). The persistence of race and gender in online interaction is highlighted by evidence that establishing the gender of participants leads to stereotypical comments and stereotypical treatment of minority groups in online interaction (Brail, 1995).

As well as the persistence of characteristics such as race and gender which constrain online participation, attention has recently been drawn to the need to consider the process by which access to the Internet can foster social inclusion. Technological literacy has been highlighted as an important constraint to the encouragement of social inclusion through new technology. Even if constraints relating to access to the technology are successfully negotiated, there are issues regarding the ability to use the technology for meaningful activities (Burrows, 2000). These findings suggest that factors identified as structural leisure constraints in leisure research, e.g., gender, race and income (Crawford *et al.* 1991) have implications for access to leisure technologies and freedom of expression and equality within virtual leisure spaces (Bryce, 2001).

Conclusions

The central theme of this paper was to address the extent to which technological developments such as the Internet and other ICTs are implicated in transforming the organization and experience of contemporary leisure practices. Based on the discussion of relevant issues in both the technology and leisure literature, it seems that the issue of the relationship between technology and changing leisure practices is complex, requiring consideration of the multiplicity of uses of technology for leisure, and how this may be implicated in blurring the traditional distinctions between active/passive, domestic/commercial etc. made in leisure research.

Issues relating to the meaning and function of leisure suggest a continuity in which new media are adopted to support and make more efficient aspects of existing leisure practices, increasing communication and sociality in leisure. In terms of changing spatial and temporal organizations of leisure, it would seem that the Internet does to an extent change these dimensions of leisure experience. It must be recognized, however, that the extent to which such changes are experienced depends on the particular online activity under consideration. These activities may be related to events in the offline world, or may be contained within the function of the particular virtual community. This demonstrates the need to consider the intersection of online, offline worlds and leisure practices. This paper has suggested other areas where boundaries related to leisure practice may become increasingly blurred. The increasing commercialization of the Internet and online shopping suggest that boundaries between domestic and commercial leisure spaces may change conceptions of consumption as leisure practice. Another important aspect of the increasing use of the Internet and ICTs is the blurring of boundaries between work and leisure, between which people may find it increasingly difficult to draw distinctions. This changing relationship also has implications for changing business practice and the psychological contract between employer and employee.

Virtual communities as the locations of online leisure practices represents an important area for future research. The organizing rationale of such communities varies widely, suggesting that individuals attach a variety of meanings to membership. Polarized debates relating to the authenticity of these communities neglects the multiple functions and organization of these new leisure spaces. The relationship between virtual communities and leisure practice requires research which moves beyond such polarization to understand community membership from the perspective of the individual user. Leisure constraints such as income, class, gender and race seem to be likely to have similar implications for access to online leisure spaces as those in offline contexts. Whilst utopian discourses claim the anonymity of cyberspace provides liberation from constraints such as these, research suggests that this is far from the case. The frequency of questions establishing the gender of virtual community members and corresponding alterations in attitude and discourse suggest that the influence of constraints persist on online contexts. Issues relating to the ability of the Internet and technology to foster social inclusion indicate the persistence of income and class as leisure constraints in contemporary society. Related to this is the need to address the issue of technological literacy and how socially excluded groups would actually use new technologies such as the Internet.

Research investigating the relationship between technology and leisure must recognize the multiplicity of leisure activities and experiences supported by the Internet and other leisure technologies. This is related to the need to study how people use technology during leisure in the context of their everyday lives. Issues relating to the meanings attached to technological leisure practices, and the relationship between online and off-line leisure activities are important areas for future research. Such research requires a multi-method and multidisciplinary approach to provide a detailed understanding of the symbolic meaning attached to online leisure practices and membership of virtual communities.

Although not specifically considered in this paper, other themes in leisure research and the technology literature have relevance to a consideration of the technology-leisure relationship. The utopian claims made for the Internet also must be considered in light of the use of technology for deviant leisure activities. Virtual communities structured around subversive, pornographic, or violent ideologies raise issues of regulation and protection for academics, government and the law (Bryce, 2001). The legality of these forms of leisure activity in cyberspace are consistent with the claim that leisure theorists need to consider the continuum of illegal and legal leisure activities in contemporary society (Rojek, 2000).

The future of the relationship between technology and leisure is likely to reflect a continuity in leisure meanings and functions, in which new technologies are adopted and utilized by individuals and groups to facilitate greater communication and sociality during leisure. One particularly important focus for future research is to consider in greater detail how the uses of other communications technologies are utilized in the experience and organization of leisure practice. Mobile phones, digital and interactive TV and gaming consoles all form part of contemporary leisure practices, and are likely to be implicated in the evolving future of leisure.

A recurrent theme throughout this paper is the need to move away from polarized discourses surrounding the relationship between the Internet, changing leisure practices, and society. Such discourses represent the Internet as a uniform and static medium having either overall positive or negative implications for society. Such discourses adopt an overly simplistic understanding of the dynamic nature of the medium and its construction by users to support a variety of activities, leisure practices and ideological expressions. The process by which the future of leisure may be shaped by new technologies and the implications of this for society indicate the need for a theoretical and empirical research incorporating relevant issues from leisure theory and literature examining the relationship between the use of ICTs and contemporary society.

Note

[1]   See http://www.brunel.ac.uk/research/virtsoc for further details.

References

Argyle, M. (1996) *The social psychology of leisure*. London: Penguin Books.

Aurigi, A. and Graham, S. (1998) 'The 'crisis' in the urban public realm', in B. D. Loader (ed) Cyberspace divide: *Equality, agency and policy in the information age*. London: Routledge, pp.156–172.

Brail, S. (1995) 'The price of admission: Harassment and free speech in the wild, wild west', in L. Cherney and E. R. Weise (eds), *Wired women*. Seattle, WA: Seal Press, pp. 141–157.

Bryce, J. (2001) 'The technological transformation of leisure', *Social Science Computer Review* Vol. 19: pp. 7–16.

Bryce, J. and Higgins, D. (2000) 'Optimal experience: A framework for the investigation of the phenomenology of computing', *Simulations and games for education and training yearbook*. London: Kogan Page, pp. 105–115.

Burkhalter, B. (1999) 'Reading race online: Discovering racial identity in Usenet groups', in M. A. Smith, and P. Kollock, *Communities in cyberspace*. London: Routledge, pp. 210–223.

Burrows, R. (2000) 'Understanding the implications of the emergence of virtual self-help for the future of welfare'. Presented at "Delivering the Virtual Promise" Conference. London: Queen Elizabeth II Conference Centre.

Castells, M. (2000) *Network society* (2nd edition). Oxford: Blackwell.

Crawford, D. W., Jackson, E. L. and Godbey, G. (1991) 'A hierarchical model of leisure constraints', *Journal of Leisure Research*, Vol. 13, pp. 309–320.

Csikszentmihalyi, M. (1975) *Beyond boredom and anxiety*. San Francisco, CA: Jossey-Bass.

Doheny-Farina, S. (1996) *The wired neighbourhood*. New Haven: Yale University Press.

ELSPA (2000) Press Release. See www.elspa.com.

Etzioni, A. (1995) 'Old chestnuts and new spurs', in A. Etzioni (ed), *New communitarian thinking: Persons, virtues, institutions and communities*. Charlottesville: University Press of Virginia, pp. 222–247.

Fernback, J. (1999) 'There is a there there: Notes towards a definition of cybercommunity', in S. Jones (ed) *Doing internet research: Issues and methods for examining the Net*. Thousand Oaks, California: Sage Publications, pp. 203–220.

Foucault, M. (1986) 'Spaces, knowledge and power', in P. Rabinow (ed), *Michel Foucault: Beyond structuralism and hermeneutics*. Harmondsworth: Penguin.

Griffths, M. (1997) 'Violent video games and aggression: A review of the literature', *Aggression and Violent Behavior*, Vol. 4: pp. 203–212.

Hine, C. (2000) *Virtual ethnography*. London: Sage Publications.

Holderness, M. (1994a) 'Welcome to the global village', *Geographical* (May). London. Royal Geographical Society.

Jones, S. G. (1998) *Cybersociety 2.0: Revisiting computer-mediated communication and community*. Thousand Oaks, CA: Sage Publications Inc.

Kabanoff, B. (1982) 'Occupational and sex differences in leisure needs and leisure satisfaction', *Journal of Occupational Behaviour*, Vol. 3, pp. 233–245.

Kendall, L. (1999) 'Recontextualizing 'cyberspace'; Methodological considerations for online research', in S. Jones (ed) *Doing internet research: Issues and methods for examining the Net*. Thousand Oaks, California: Sage Publications, pp.57–74.

Kendall, L. (1998) 'Are you male or female?', in J. Ollgen and J. Howard (eds), *Everyday inequalities: Critical enquiries*. London: Basil Blackwell, pp.131–135.

Kling, R. (1996) 'Social relations in electronic forums: Hangouts, salons, workplaces, and communities', in R. King (ed), *Computerization and controversy: Value conflicts and social choices* (2nd edition). San Diego, CA: Academic Press, pp. 426–454.

Langford, D. (1998) 'Ethics @ the Internet: Bilateral procedures in electronic communication', in B. D. Loader. (ed), *Cyberspace divide: Equality, agency and policy in the information age*. London: Routledge, pp. 89–101.

Lansbury, M. (2000) '2e or not 2e? The possibility of e-tailing', Paper presented at "The Future of Consumer E-commerce" Conference. London: Consumers Association (date?).

Neulinger, J. (1974) *The psychology of leisure*. Springfield, IL: Charles C. Thomas.

Nie, N. H. and Erbring, L. (2000) *Internet and society: A preliminary report*. Stanford: Stanford Institute for the Quantitative Study of Society.

O'Brien, J. (1999) 'Writing in the body: Gender (re)production in online interaction', in M. A. Smith P. and Kollock (eds) *Communities in cyberspace*. London: Routledge.

The Retail E-commerce Task Force (2000) *Clicks and mortar*.UK: DTI.

Rheingold, H. (1993) 'A slice of life in my virtual community', in L. M. Harasim (ed), *Global networks*. Cambridge: MIT Press.

Rojek, C. (1995) *Decentring leisure*. London: Sage.

———— (2000) *Leisure and culture*. UK: Macmillan Press Limited.

Rutter, J. and Southerton, D. (2000) 'E-commerce: the benefits for consumers?' Paper presented at "The Future of Consumer" E-commerce Conference. London: Consumers Association (June).

Slevin, J. (2000) *The internet and society*. Great Britain: Polity Press

Schuler, D. (1996) *New community networks: Wired for change*. Reading, MA: Addison-Wesley.

Smith, M. A. and Kollock, P. (1999) *Communities in cyberspace*. London: Routledge.

Stebbins, R. A. (1997) 'Casual leisure: A conceptual statement', *Leisure Studies*, Vol. 16, No. 1: pp. 17–25.

Stebbins, R. A. (1982) 'Serious leisure: a conceptual statement', *Pacific Sociological Review*, Vol. 25: pp. 251–272.

Wellman, B. and Gullia, M. (1999) 'Virtual communities as communities: Net surfers don't ride alone', in M. A. Smith and P. Kollock (eds), *Communities in cyberspace*. London: Routledge, pp.10–21.

Winston, B. (1998) *Media, technology and society, a history: From telegraph to internet*. London: Routledge.

Woolgar, S. (2000) 'Defining the digital divide'. Paper presented at Citizens Online. London: BAFTA.

Yates, S. J. and Littleton, K. (1998) 'Understanding computer game cultures: A situated approach'. *Information, Communication and Society* Vol. 2: pp. 566–583.

Part Two:

Consumption, Culture and Heritage

Brand Images of Place and New Urban Identities in Scotland: The Case of Dundee, The City of Discovery

MariaLaura Di Domenico

University of Abertay Dundee, and University of Strathclyde in Glasgow

Introduction

Dundee is an interesting example of a British town that has been going through numerous changes throughout its history. During the 1970s, 1980s and 1990s, Dundee suffered from continued economic decline. By then, most of the jute factories had finally closed down along with other associated industries. The bitter dispute in 1993 surrounding the closure of the multinational company, Timex, was a clear marker highlighting the decline in Dundee's manufacturing industries. This conflict was particularly important to the city not only from an economic but also from a symbolic perspective. This was partly due to the role of Timex, along with other light engineering industries, in providing, not only employment in post World War II Dundee, but also a sense of identity and hope for the city's future during that period.

The rising unemployment in Dundee since the early 1970s does not seem to have led most of its citizens towards despair for the future. Instead, there was greater commitment on the part of policy makers to the strategy of urban change in Dundee with a focus on other areas of development such as tourism, teaching and high-tech industries. The Discovery Point Heritage Centre, with Captain Scott's ship The Discovery, symbolises the city's new hope for the future. It is through the image, which the concept of discovery paints for the public, that the city has attempted to build a new identity over the past decade, although based on a pastiche of former identities. This new image reflects a city which is innovative and forward looking rather than an industrial city in decline. The strategy is to make the title, City of Discovery, synonymous with the new Dundee. It involves an attempt to repackage and market the city more attractively, directing efforts to interpretations of the perspectives of tourists as well as residents.

The maritime heritage industry which is being developed must therefore be seen both in relation to the city's actual history as well as to the present context of urban regeneration and the re-imaging of Dundee. The city is now in the process of being converted into a centre with a maritime heritage focus through its new brand image as the City of Discovery. Policy makers intend that the development of the maritime heritage tourism industry and the focus on the ship, The Discovery, combined with the regeneration of the city centre, will eventually be the pivot around which the success of Dundee's tourism industry will evolve. This, it is hoped, will contribute to the development of a new and broader economic base for the city.

The research discussed in this paper involves an analysis of some recent changes connected to the tourism and heritage industries against a late 1990s backdrop of the evolving face of Dundee city centre. A research focus is the work of the Dundee Heritage Trust, and its main tourist attraction, Discovery Point, which has been open to the public for almost five years. Further development of the maritime heritage industry would appear important, not only to the success of the tourism industry, but also as part of the urban regeneration programme of the city. However, as McCrone *et al.* (1995) show, the heritage industry often provides information and entertainment or "infotainment" rather than history. Much can be learnt if research is conducted into particular case studies, such as this one of Dundee, placing the analysis within a broad theoretical account of the Scottish heritage industry.

Maritime heritage cultural tourism in the Scottish urban setting

Heritage research involves the analysis of how the conservation of history is turned into a modern commodity, a heritage product for contemporary consumption. Heritage can be identified as a mixture of "history, ideology, nationalism, local pride, romantic ideas or just plain marketing" (Herbert, 1995: p. 56). Scottish cultural heritage can be said to involve symbolic meanings and purpose, reinforcing a sense of group belonging and national cultural identity. Symbols associated with tradition and heritage are in reality a complex reconstruction of fact and fiction, helping to give Scots a sense of shared identity during periods of social, economic and political change. The word heritage covers a range of subjects, including a variety of material and symbolic inheritance, and acts as "a vital source of legitimatory iconography" (McCrone *et al.*, 1995: p. 5). Many local authorities, like Dundee, have developed a range of historical and heritage services, in their attempt to attract educational tourists eager to learn about heritage, home and history. This has become an important area of investment and employment, and a source of jobs and income. Witt and Moutinho cite the "wide range of purpose-built, managed visitor attractions" as a "primary motivation for tourist visits" (1995: p. 335). Such developments are marketable "tourist commodities" producing generally attractive images of the industrial past for the areas in which they are situated (Abercrombie and Warde, 1994: p. 336). Maritime heritage like cultural heritage is concerned with the conservation and restoration of the past, preserving an important version of identity and history. Maritime heritage tourism focuses attention on the reciprocal influences between tourism and maritime heritage. Scottish maritime heritage represents and strengthens certain aspects of national and cultural identity and appears to be an important development area in tourism which could attract visitors. Edinburgh has recently invested, for example, in bringing The Britannia to Leith. Likewise Dundee's once thriving shipbuilding and whaling industries have given the city the opportunity to develop this area of tourism. Maritime museums such as Discovery Point draw attention to a sea-faring past deemed worthy of preservation. However, as is shown below, this is only one part of Dundee's past and a part which many feel has been emphasised at the expense of other aspects of the city's urban and industrial heritage.

Urban heritage tourism has developed recently in Scotland as a whole, reflecting the fact that many cities are now tourist attractions in their own right, with a variety of projections of heritage, history and culture. Indeed, cities, as centres of transportation networks allowing ease of access to other surrounding locations, have tended to be focal points of tourist concentration and diversity. In Scotland as elsewhere in the UK, city-based cultural and heritage services are becoming increasingly attractive and industrial centres now compete with older cultural centres. For example, Dundee competes with other nearby cities in Scotland for the opportunity to act as a honey pot in the provision of a diverse range of social, cultural and economic activities, including tourism, leisure and entertainment services. The heritage re-imaging effect, which many cities have undergone recently, involving urban regeneration and the conservation of old buildings, including docks, presents us with a townscape of the city as a heritage centre complete with cultural quarters. However, the heritage industry involves commerce as well as culture. Corner and Harvey (1991) describe the mixture of public and private interests as an interconnectedness of heritage with ideas of enterprises such as the shops and restaurants in cleaned-up areas. Thus, Dundee may be taken as a prime example of such cities, as it is actively exploiting its maritime past, having acquired The Discovery very cheaply from the Greater London council as it was being closed down. For Dundee as for many other cities, tourism, urban regeneration and economic diversification can be seen to have gone hand in hand.

The variety and recent increase in heritage tourism in Scotland is reflected in the growth of heritage-based museums and related centres throughout the country. They cover subjects ranging from the Loch Ness Monster Exhibition in Drumnadrochit and the clan tartan centres found throughout the Highlands (Rosie, 1992) to the maritime heritage museum at Discovery Point. Walsh (1992) echoes the argument of McCrone *et al.* (1995), when referring to the heritage boom at home and abroad which has exploded over the last twenty years. Morris *et al.* (1995) point out that, out of four hundred museums in Scotland, half of these have opened since the 1970s. This may be a reflection of an increasing awareness of Scotland's heritage and the need to designate the existence of places and artifacts once ignored. It also shows a growing interest or demand for heritage tourism in Scotland among residents as well as visitors, partly as a result of increasing awareness of the power of Scottish imagery to promote tourism.

The recent emphasis on heritage tourism in Scotland reflects also a drive towards the discovery of their own heritage on the part of Scottish people. Despite this, the emphasis is usually more on natural heritage or scenery rather than man-made artifacts. Maritime heritage tourism relies on the natural element of the sea combined with the role of nostalgia in order to have an impact on people. That involves a selective remembering of aspects of history and the romanticising of reality. This appears to be a powerful factor in general in creating an interest in Scotland as a tourist destination. Walsh (1992) argues that the heritage industry relies on nostalgia through the portrayal of selective images in heritage centres which give their own representation in a romantic version of the past, often ignoring less presentable aspects of history. The danger is that Scottish culture and heritage are evolving into branded and idealised images, especially in relation to the heritage industry. The potential consumer is presented with typical themes or brands. Gold and Gold (1995) examine "imagining Scotland" in the representation of Scotland to the outside world in tourist-promotional literature and related media, examining the selling of urban Scotland through the promotion of heritage. The end result may be far removed from actual events or happenings. However, it is ironic that it is perhaps this imagining which gives history and culture its critical appeal to the tourist, and indeed the Scot, in search for a culture and identity.

In this context, it is important to consider further the views of David McCrone *et al.* (1995) who present a sociological account of the rise of Scottish heritage, examining four themes. Firstly, the commodification of heritage is examined. This is mobilised more and more by private and public capital and the fudging of the distinction between commerce and heritage (McCrone *et al.*, 1995: p. 41). Shops now resemble museums and museums have become shops. Higher charges are being sought for entry to museums and heritage centres such as Discovery Point, redefined as for "infotainment" which should be paid for rather than education which could be free. Secondly, the consumption of heritage pertains to the transition from a manufacturing to a service-based economy, which brings the consumption of culture and heritage to the fore. Thirdly, heritage can be linked to culture and politics presented as indivisible and conservative, as a Scottish nationalist heritage. Finally, in Baudrillard's terms, the ideology of heritage is "where the real is no longer the real". This leads us to the argument that the past is an imaginary object (McCrone *et al.*, 1995: pp. 25 and 39) and the assumption that Scottish national culture is tied up in myths, romantic ideals and history. History is the bold fact of an event whereas heritage is the romantic interpretation of the past. Dundee can be seen to be now actively exploiting its maritime history, as opposed to its other possible histories, in order to develop a heritage industry for a future built on a selective reinterpretation of the past.

In portraying the growth of the Scottish heritage industry, some commentators feel that instead of moving forward and innovating, we may be simply falling back on heritage which may be detrimental to the nation in a wider sense. For instance, the journalist Victoria Glendinning stated that "with no-one now to boss around, we fall back on 'heritage' … We are the world's ingrowing toenail" (Glendinning, 1997: p. 12). Fears have also been expressed in the press by academics such as Professor Devine who states that Scotland's "heritage is being hijacked and repackaged for the instant consumer market at the expense of serious historical study" (quoted by Carlos Abba, 1997: p. 7). However, despite his demands for consistent authenticity and a rejection of what he perceives to be a distortion of reality, he still concedes that many themes are important in a financial sense. It may be said that: "The question is not whether we should or should not preserve the past, but what kind of past we have chosen to preserve" (Urry, 1990: p. 109). In Dundee's case, as the City of Discovery, it includes a maritime past. In this era of Scottish devolution, maritime heritage for Dundee, like memory for the individual, presents a narrative which can be continually interpreted and re-interpreted. This allows a development of themes, such as those of discovery, innovation, research and exploration, which are ever more necessary in a rapidly changing world, re-injecting into Dundonians a feeling of pride and identity in their city. The idea of developing and constructing a present identity from the maritime past of Dundee is one that is in the process of taking physical shape and this in turn may help to redefine the city for its inhabitants and those who visit. However, if we examine Dundee's history and background, doubts must remain about the legitimacy of this endeavour.

Dundee's background

Dundee grew rapidly from a medium size town in the nineteenth century to Scotland's fourth largest city in the twentieth century. This was due first of all to its location at the mouth of the River Tay, looking out to the North Sea and with land suitable for building docks which encouraged the transportation of goods. Secondly, it was due to the Industrial Revolution which led to the establishment of the linen and jute industries followed by other industries such as jam and journalism and the subsequent immigration of workers into Dundee resulting in the growth of the population. However, especially after the Second World War, there was a continued decline in the jute industry.

Dundee's decline was for some years masked by the continued prosperity of other manufacturing industries, mainly the multinationals which had been established in the post-war era making use of middle level technology. Approximately 10,000 people, or about 12% of Dundee's occupied population found employment in these companies and for the first time in Dundee's history employment in textiles was overtaken by employment in light engineering. The case of Timex is a good example of such an industry, as is NCR (National Cash Registers) which still operates in the city. The post-war optimism engendered was sustained throughout the 1960s. However, the 1970s saw an end to post-war growth throughout the country and Dundee suffered an economic crisis with a steady contraction of its manufacturing base due partly to increased global competition. The postwar industries went into decline, resulting in high unemployment in the city. This was linked to a decline in Dundee's population size after 1971. This decline in population had many consequences for the city. For example, its population distribution and density were affected. These all had further implications for the city's environment, access and transportation. At this point, the image of Dundee as Juteopolis was almost dead. Another myth of Dundee as Scotland's forgotten city began to emerge. Indeed, Dundee was not only not Scotland's industrial city par excellence as it had been before, but no longer even a predominantly manufacturing city. Service industries rather than manufacturing now account for a higher proportion of employment. This is a trend that has continued up until the present.

It is ironic that the once proud Juteopolis is now no more than an image in a Dundee heritage museum, Verdant Works: "The great bales of hemp which were carried halfway around the world from India were modern Dundee's first strength — and its greatest weakness" (Ogilvy, 1993: p. 36). The last bale of jute was delivered to Dundee in 1998 to this museum where the visitor is asked to step back in time and to imagine the jute worker of about one hundred years ago. The Verdant Works exhibition highlights how typical jute workers tended to be women. Indeed, women in jute manufacture outnumbered men by at least two to one. As far back as the Census Report of 1901, it was shown that "Dundee had more than half its women at work" (Butt, 1985: p. 213). In 1901, for example, of the 39,752 workers employed in textiles in Dundee, two-thirds were female. "More than any of the other Scottish cities, Dundee had the image of being a 'woman's town' rather than a city where men could obtain employment. Nowhere was this seen more clearly than in the formal world of work" (Whatley, 1992: p. 7). At work in the mills, women and children were often the preferred choice by the jute barons as they were seen as generally more manageable and "if men got the working ... they might strike" (Walker, 1979: p. 34). However, the women workers of that era also had a tradition of resilience: "Verbatim newspaper reports of speeches given at that time give a picture of women being openly scathing about their employers — 'You know some of them are just set up with a little authority and they think they have the ball at their feet and they can kick it any way they like'" (quoted in Henderson, 1997: p. 2). However, the importance of skilled female labour frequently did entail comparatively lower wages for all, as well as fewer employment opportunities for the men, who endured long periods of unemployment, and thus became known locally as kettle boilers. Work in ship-building and on the docks did not offer men the work that it offered to the women in the jute industry. This established female work tradition in Dundee was to continue with post-war employment patterns in companies such as Timex and as a trend up until the present.

The setting up of the Verdant Works converted jute mill heritage museum in 1996 was planned ten years earlier by Dundee Heritage Trust to represent Dundee's industrial heritage as part of the Dundee Project. In response to the decline of manufacturing, in the late 1980s and 1990s policy makers in Dundee adopted various strategies for boosting the city's image by promoting the three Ts of teaching, tourism and technology in contrast to the three Js of jute, jam and journalism, for which the city was once famous. Indeed, the Dundee Project was first launched in 1982 in an effort to save the city from economic decline and to change its image from that of Juteopolis, one that still prevailed up until that time. This image was still present then, despite the post-war decline in the jute industry and the subsequent economic and social changes that had taken place in the city.

The Dundee Project was an attempt to repackage and market the city more attractively. However, despite such efforts, an apparent economic, social and psychological depth was reached in the city in the early 1990s, and especially in 1993, which was symbolised by the bitter Timex dispute. At that time, the rise and fall of Timex was seen to have had an important effect on the city's economic future, and so on all its citizens, as well as particularly on the women who once worked there. The collapse of Timex was particularly important both from a symbolic perspective, given its role in providing employment in post World War II Dundee, and especially in the 1970s when other industries were in decline. The closure of Timex in 1993 was a watershed for the citizens of Dundee. This put the city's industrial decline into national headlines with images depicting the mainly women workers, their trade union leaders and their confrontation with the police on the picket lines. These images shown in 1993 were in stark contrast to other images of The Discovery being presented to the outside world in the same year. The launching of the Dundee Project had been followed by a promotional campaign aiming to brand Dundee as the City of Discovery after Captain's Scott's ship, The Discovery, which had been built in Dundee. In 1993, it was being berthed on Discovery Quay at the purpose-built Discovery Point museum, heritage and conference centre opened in the same period of 1993 as the Timex dispute hit the headlines. Discovery Point, now a tourist attraction, focuses on the shipbuilding past of Dundee in the nineteenth century, when the city was a centre for whaling and ship building and possessed a merchant fleet that was later to keep the town's industries supplied with raw materials. The Discovery makes a striking feature at the main western route into the city centre. However, it presents only one facet of Dundee's story and is in sharp contrast to the other stories which could have been told around the history of the women workers of the city.

Dundonians have a history of resilience in the face of hardship and since 1993, as well as despondency following the closure of the Timex factory, there appears to have been an equal and increased determination to boost the city's image along the lines symbolised by The Discovery. Decision-makers in the city have been stimulated towards even more commitment to the strategies involved in urban change and tourism in their efforts to re-image Scotland's former premier industrial city, once associated with jute, but now with the brand image of Discovery always kept in mind. This place boosterism, which is becoming increasingly common in Britain, has been a focus of development in other Scottish cities as well as Dundee, and especially in those that suffered from post-industrial decline. In Dundee the images of place being presented to the public have involved a conscious effort to promote certain aspects of the city's history and identity while downplaying others which may be thought to be less attractive to investors and tourists. One aspect, which has been sidetracked in this way, has been the city's history of left-wing militancy and trade unionism. Another is Dundee's increasing Janus-faced divide into two cities where one face looks forward to a high-tech future and the other back to an era of industrial decline and despair.

Dundee's maritime past, preserved and marketed in the present for the future

The Discovery Point project is managed and marketed by Dundee Industrial Heritage Ltd. which originally commissioned the building which was mainly financed by Scottish Enterprise Tayside at a cost of £6m in a bid to boost the economic and environmental development of Dundee city centre. However, certain questions remain to be answered. Has the project succeeded? How important is the ship itself in terms of historical significance and maritime heritage conservation? Is it merely an icon or is it indeed an important heritage asset?

The Statement of Significance in RRS Discovery's Conservation Plan must be examined as it highlights the ship's historical, heritage and other contributions to the city and nation. Its uniqueness is explained by the fact that it is described as a leader in exploration and research. It is further argued that this gives it an international status in being the originator of scientific maritime and specialist terrestrial ship-based research. It is also argued that it was the first ship in the world to be designed specifically for scientific research and was part of the first extensive scientific exploration of the Antarctic land mass. It is again presented as a part of the first maritime research undertaken to explore the natural habitat of the whale and the exploitation of the mammal as a resource. As such, it was part of extensive surveys and biological research of the landmasses and oceans of the South Atlantic and Antarctic. It is also marketed as one of the last wooden three-masted sailing ships to be built in Britain and the only surviving example of traditional Scottish wooden whaling ships which was used in the ice-packed areas of the North Pole. Consequently, for all these reasons, it is argued that it is an important heritage asset. However much all these features are important, it is also pointed out in that they contribute considerably, not only to the development of a valuable local and national educational facility, but also to tourism and the local economy of Dundee.

According to the marketing literature and brochures available, the tourist experience of this attraction is intended to be not only educational but also entertaining and clearly interactive involving "spectacular exhibits and special effects" which recreate "the historic voyages of Captain Scott's Antarctic ship, Royal Research Ship Discovery". The tourist is invited to "absorb the sights, sounds and smells of the ship-yard. Cheer as she is launched. Then sit back and enjoy 'Locked in the Ice', a dramatic presentation on three giant screens showing how Discovery was blasted free from the crushing pack ice. Across the quayside you can board and explore Discovery herself, probably the strongest wooden ship ever built, now restored as she was on her last great adventure" (Discovery Point, 1997). In this way, the RRS Discovery is presented as an important historical artifact, an educational tool and also a source of entertainment for the visitor. At the same time, it is being used both as a marketing tool and as an aesthetic symbol, in the quest for urban and economic regeneration of the city of Dundee.

It was argued strongly by its developers in the Dundee Heritage Trust when interviewed that Discovery Point is being conserved and marketed as an important part of Dundee's historical heritage in its own right. However, in addition, they agree that it is also being developed as Dundee's main visitor attraction. Furthermore, they affirm that it symbolises the envisaged rebirth of the city with the concept of discovery as its theme. Nevertheless, on a national level, they admit that it may only be categorised as a medium-scale attraction only, due to the relatively low level of tourist numbers for which it currently caters. Thus although "visitor numbers to Discovery Point have grown from 75,000 in 1993 to 114,000 visitors in 1994", they "are still disappointing in terms of earlier expectations and levels required for operational viability" (Dundee Visitor Attractions Strategic Review: 1996: pp. 21–22). The main catchment area from which this attraction draws most of its patrons is approximately one to two hours driving distance away. The Marketing Manager of the Dundee Heritage Trust, Alan Rankin, stresses this point. There has been "adopted a geographical emphasis, whereby the Central Belt has been targeted, and anywhere within a 50-mile radius of Discovery Point is seen as a possible new market". It must be added that "the quality of the concept presentation is impressive but given the available marketing budget of around £110,000 p.a., both the volume of visitor admissions to the centre and the market awareness of the attraction is disappointing. As a result, there is a recognition that further product development is required if the level of visitor numbers is to increase substantially. Such development should be much more market than 'theme' led and related to its target markets" (Dundee Visitor Attractions Strategic Review: 1996: p. 22.)

The way ahead?

The present research was undertaken in Dundee which over the last decade has undergone dramatic restructuring and like other Western cities has "adapted to new economic, social and political realities" (Hubbard, 1996: p. 26). Heritage tourism in Dundee has been increasingly recognised as an identifiable sector and one of the city's recent growth industries. Prentice (1993) identifies the surge in local initiatives to promote local economic redevelopment and the heritage resources of a particular place. However, in the case of Dundee, certain heritage resources of the industrial past have been emphasised more than others. This is symbolised by the jute museum, Verdant Works, which seems to be less attractive to visitors than Discovery Point, which in turn has been given more emphasis by the city. Both museums do, however, fit in to a romanticised view of Dundee's past. However, the more recent manufacturing past of the post-war era, which is reflected in the Timex dispute, appears to be one that was to be avoided in a retrospective view of the city as it clashed with this more romanticised version of Dundee's history.

Thus, heritage is seen in Dundee as a core component in the revitalisation strategy leading to economic regeneration. We cannot yet say whether Dundee will succeed in this strategy and reverse the tide of decline. However, one could end on a positive note with the words of Charles Handy — philosopher, management thinker and founder of the London Business School — who is quoted in the 'Dundee Courier and Advertiser' as having singled out the City of Discovery for high praise. Handy it is said suggests that the world needs 'more Dundees' if it is to fulfil Adam Smith's vision of societies as places of cultivation where economic and cultural growth are inextricably linked. He is quoted as saying that "Dundee — a dour town in the east of Scotland noted in the past for jam and jute — is seeking to reinvent itself ... It may prove too small to become a real cluster of alchemy but it is certainly going the right way about it" (Anon, 2000: p. 4).

Finally, therefore, it can be stated that, despite all the misgivings about the commodification of Scottish history when transformed into maritime heritage attractions such as Discovery Point in Dundee, we can go some way in endorsing Dundee's efforts and attempts to re-image itself. It is a valiant attempt to save itself from drowning in the post-industrial age by looking to its maritime heritage for its salvation. Thus, Dundee's maritime heritage confirms Professor Tom Devine's view that we must look to our collective heritage as Scottish people. We can further hope that the aim of Dundee in this new era of its development will be to make sure that "the future is good for Scots past" (Wojtas, 1998: p. 6).

References

Abba, C. (1997) 'Fears over hijacked heritage', *The Herald,* (Glasgow) 14th August: p. 7.

Abercrombie, N. and Warde, A. (1994) *Contemporary British society*. Cambridge: Polity Press.

Anon (2000) City of Discovery Praised as Model of Re-invention', *The Courier and Advertiser* (Dundee), 14th February: p. 4.

Butt, J. (1985) 'The changing character of urban employment: 1901–1981', in G. Gordon (ed) *Perspectives of the Scottish city*. Aberdeen: Aberdeen University Press, (pp. 212–235).

Corner, J. and Harvey, S. (eds) (1991) *Enterprise and heritage*. London: Routledge.

Discovery Point (1997) Brochure: pp. 1–12.

Dundee Visitor Attractions Strategic Review: Final Report: January 1996.

Glendinning, V. (1997) Untitled article, *The Sunday Telegraph* (London), 13th June: p. 12.

Gold, J. R. and Gold, M. M. (1995). *Imagining Scotland: Tradition, representation and promotion in Scottish tourism since 1750*. Aldershot: Scolar Press 1995.

Henderson, M. (1997) *Dundee Women's Achievement Trail*. Dundee: Dundee City Council Women's Forum.

Herbert, D. (1995) 'Heritage as literary place', in D. Herbert (ed) *Heritage, tourism and society*. London: Mansell, pp. 32–48.

Hubbard, P. (1996) 'Re-imaging the City', *Geography* Vol. 81, No. 1: pp. 26–36.

McCrone, D., Morris, A. and Kiely, R. (1995) *Scotland — the brand: The making of Scottish heritage*. Edinburgh: Edinburgh University Press.

Morris, A., McCrone, D. and Kiely, R. (1995) 'The heritage consumers: Identity and affiliations in Scotland', in J. M. Fladmark (ed) *Sharing the earth: Local identity in global culture*. London: Donhead.

Ogilvy, G. (1993) *The River Tay and its people*. Edinburgh: Mainstream Publishing.

Prentice, R.C. (1993). *Tourism and heritage attractions*. London: Routledge.

Rosie, G. (1992) Museumry and the heritage industry', in J. Donnachie and C. Whatley (eds) *The manufacture of Scottish History*. Edinburgh: Polygon.

Urry, J. (1990) *The tourist gaze: Leisure and travel in contemporary societies*. London: Sage.

Walker, W. M. (1979) *Juteopolis: Dundee and its textile workers 1885–1923*. Edinburgh: Scottish Academic Press.

Walsh, K. (1992) *The representation of the past: Museums and heritage in the post-modern world*. London: Routledge.

Whatley, C. (1992) 'The making of 'Juteopolis' — and how it was', in C. Whatley (ed) *The remaking of Juteopolis: Dundee circa 1891–1991*. Dundee: Abertay Historical Society Publication No. 32, pp. 7–22.

Witt, S. F., and Moutinho, L. (eds) (1995) *Tourism marketing and management handbook* (2nd Edition). Hemel Hempstead: Prentice Hall International (UK) Limited.

Wojtas, O. (1998) 'Future is good for Scots past', *The Times Higher Education Supplement* (London), 27th February: p. 6.

Tourism Games and the Commodification of Tradition

Eleanor Lothian

School of Social and Health Sciences
University of Abertay Dundee

Introduction

In 1991, Jarvie published *The Highland Games: the Making of the Myth*. In this work, he presented an analysis of the development of Scottish highland gatherings and distinguished four interrelated stages of development. In this paper, the proposition is put forward that, from around 1980, a fifth stage has become discernible and that this can be referred to as the tourism games stage. However, this is not a straightforward proposition, as during this era two types of games appear to have emerged, the traditional games and the tourism games. For the purpose of this paper, tourism games are defined as those which have been introduced, revived or regenerated since around 1980 with an important objective being to attract tourists to the area. Traditional games were introduced prior to this, mostly during the nineteenth century and application of this fifth stage may not be relevant to some or all of them. Applying this rudimentary classification to the 15 highland games known to have taken place in Tayside during 1998, over 50% fall into the category of tourism games. In this paper, an attempt is made to explain why this proliferation has taken place by examining tourism marketing and performance and also to determine whether these tourism games were developed to satisfy the new 'culture hungry' consumer. A further attempt is made to determine and assess the extent to which tourism games could be said to reflect a commodification of traditional events in order to satisfy the expectations of the twenty-first century tourist.

Historical context — the preceding eras

Jarvie's analysis of Highland Games identifies four eras in the development of sport that are viewed within the context of history and social development (Jarvie, 1991).

93

Providing explanations and distinguishing features for a fifth era, the tourism games, is not possible without reference to the past. The following paragraphs highlight and expand only the parts relevant to this study and as such, this section is neither intended to give a new sense of direction to Jarvie's work nor to summarise his work in this area per se. However, the analysis presented in this paper is built on a foundation which owes much to Jarvie's initial insights.

The first era lasted from the eleventh century until about 1750. During this time, many of the origins of today's highland gatherings emerged, including running, playing the piobaieachd, dancing and wearing highland dress. Games occurred largely in the highlands, the first took place in Braemar, which can trace its origins back to the 11th century. At this time, land in the highlands, under the clan system, was the property of the clansfolk.

The second era took place between 1740 and 1850, which saw both the Act of Proscription (1747) and its Repeal (1782). After Culloden, highland dress, gatherings, playing bagpipes and carrying arms were banned. The clan system was repressed and the powers of the chiefs removed. The Highland Clearances and migration that took place during this time are infamous. A powerful landowner class replaced the clan chiefs and began to fill the vacant hills with sheep. At the same time, they sought to preserve a distorted form of the highland way of life. Largely responsible for the Repeal, together with Sir Walter Scott, they selected and created the cultural symbols of Scottish identity such as the kilt.

It was towards the end of this era that one of the greatest achievements in desti-nation branding of all times took place —albeit inadvertently, for it was meant for political ends rather than tourism promotion — the invention of the highland tradition by Sir Walter Scott. Responsible for much of the romantic literature that served to 'tutor' the tourist gaze, Scott was made Master of Ceremonies for the visit of George IV to Edinburgh in 1822. This was the first time the monarch had visited Scotland since 1633 and the visit was devised to improve loyalty to the government and the standing of the monarchy. Although Scott's name does not feature to a great extent in the liter-ature around highland games, his actions and their development are inextricably linked. According to Gold and Gold, the King's visit to Edinburgh provided Scott with the opportunity to introduce an identity for the whole of Scotland, based largely around the one recently created for the highlands. This can be seen as his greatest work of fiction. Jacobites and Hanovarians were united and people were advised about costume and etiquette under Scott's revised highland identity. He presented a "national unity literally cast in highland clothing" (1995: p. 73). The kilted George IV, was recognised as being a descendant of Robert the Bruce and all Scots, on becoming Highlanders could claim to belong to the clans, the landowners emerging as clan chiefs (now the Patrons and Chieftains of present-day games).

The third era took place between 1850 and 1920. During this period the spread of the games was fuelled by a "Glorification of the Highlands" when, legitimised by

Queen Victoria, the highlands became the sporting playgrounds of the elite, many of who chose to emulate the tartan wearing royalty and their fascination with the highlands, particularly highland games. It was during this phase that the wearing of highland dress for competitors at some games was made compulsory and "accessories that would have struck the old highland clansfolk as amazing were incorporated into the outfit" (p. 103). Many of the competitions were restricted (to "gentlemen") as were the social aspects, such as the highland balls. The need to introduce the Crofters Act (1886) informs us that the social relationship between tenants and landowners was far from harmonious.

The final era dates from around 1920 when, during the 1920s and 30s a "golden era" was noted. In Airth "crowds of over 10,000 regularly watched competitors compete" and the extension of the programme to include "popular working class Lowland sports like whippet racing and pony trotting". After the second world war, attendances and finances fluctuated as games had to compete with other forms of entertainment and the contribution of tourism and sponsorship became increasingly important in the survival of many. Bureaucracies, such as the Scottish Games Association were established to regulate and standardise competitions.

Many of these legacies are evident in Highland games today. At almost all games landowners double as Chieftains or Patrons, some host clan gatherings and competitors are expected to wear highland dress. In some cases, there is evidence that the relationship between the Chieftain and the "Clansfolk" has not changed much, as seen from this inclusion in the 1996 Program of the 127th Gathering of the Glenisla Highland and Friendly Society:

> We are greatly indebted to our local landlords, and to the many descendants of our original glen families, who attend our games regularly, and whose generosity helps make the Gathering such a successful occasion.

Scottish tourism

Key elements of Scotland's appeal to international visitors are history, heritage and culture, and include familiar icons such as whisky, tartan and highland dancing/games (Scottish Tourist Board: undated). Attending highland games is probably seen by visitors to be one of the most the most quintessentially Scottish experiences which is both readily available and easily accessible throughout Scotland. They take place in highland and lowland and urban and rural settings. The web site of the Scottish Tourist Board, holiday.scotland.net, lists 161 highland games and gatherings that are scheduled to take place throughout Scotland during 2000. However of these, only 117 offer the full three sets of competition — heavy field events, highland dancing and running — that enables them to be considered "proper" highland games.

Despite acknowledging the importance of these icons, recent years have seen the Tourist Board favour instead scenery and space, introducing tourists to a rugged, desolate Scotland in the promotional literature. In a recent overseas brochure, tartan and people have been played down to the extent that tartan is only noticeable on the front cover and, of the 31 main photographic illustrations, people are present in only 9. Of the 79 events listed, 6 are highland games. The brochure sent to potential visitors from the UK has a much stronger emphasis on history, people and activities. However, the use of landscape is still significant and again, the brochure is largely tartanless. Out of 46 events, the Millennium Highland Gathering and Games Championships in the Black Isle are the only highland games listed.

In recent years, growth in Scottish tourism has failed to keep abreast with growth in world tourism and in addition, tourism in Scotland has become increasingly spatially concentrated. As the Scottish Tourist Board notes, while expenditure in Edinburgh and Glasgow is growing, a similar pattern in the remainder of Scotland has not taken place. In 1997, for example, growth in Edinburgh and Glasgow was 5% while growth in the rest of Scotland was 1% (1998). The Tourist Board recognise that there is a need to grow tourism throughout Scotland while "meeting customer demand, managing over-demand and highlighting lesser known areas", as "tourism is more important to the economy of remoter areas" (1999: p. 9). In 1997 for example, while tourism accounted for 7% of employment in Glasgow and 8% in Edinburgh, in Perthshire 13% of jobs relied on the industry. In many rural areas tourism is a vital, and often underestimated, part of the economy.

The part of Scotland known as Tayside was defined by the creation of regional government in 1974, and comprises the counties of Angus and Perth and Kinross and includes the cities of Dundee and Perth. The region has a diverse topography and the popular tourist route from Edinburgh to Inverness, the A9, passes through the region, enabling parts of Perthshire to develop as successful tourist areas. It has several long established attractions, including Glamis Castle and Scone Palace as well as world famous golf courses. Recently, new attractions have opened such as RRS Discovery and Verdant Works in Dundee, Pictavia in Angus and Perth Agricultural Centre. New hotels have opened in and around the main cities of Dundee and Perth (notably larger units that are part of a chain). Yet during 1995 a 7% decrease in the total number of tourism related businesses were recorded in Angus (Tayside Economic Research Centre, 1999) and these closures are likely to be due a reduction in visitor expenditure. Overseas spending for example, decreased by around 28% between 1996 – 97 and spending by domestic tourists decreased by 5% in both Angus and Perthshire from 1991–97 (Scottish Enterprise Tayside, 2000).

This is not a phenomenon of the late 1990s. Arrivals to Scotland (i.e. rest of UK plus international arrivals) have declined by 2.2% per annum from 1985 to 1994. There has also been a large reduction in the number of Scots taking holidays at home, which fell from 6.6 million in 1985 to 4.4 million in 1994 (Seaton and Hayes, 1998). The situation does not look likely to change this year with a 10% drop in visitors to date (Gray, 2000). Several explanations are put forward for this, the most recent being the cost of fuel, poor service and the strength of the pound. In addition, the cost of internal flights is prohibitive. Writing in the Scotsman, Morton notes "Air fares within Scotland are at a level which simply beggars belief. It is possible for a couple to fly to New York and back for the price of a single return between Glasgow and Shetland. You can have an entire two-week holiday in Tenerife for the same money" (2000: p. 5). The situation therefore is one of 'low' or 'no' growth. It is against this background of decline that the late twentieth century surge in "tourism" games in Scotland should be considered.

Producing and consuming tourism

In the development of leisure tourism products the consumer is king. Hall refers to Harvey to point out that "Postmodernism ... signals nothing more than a logical extension of the power of the market over the whole range of cultural production" (1994: p. 188). Hughes notes that this modern marketing approach "lies in its customer orientation" and that in order to achieve profitable sales and satisfactory returns on investment customer needs have to be identified, anticipated and satisfied. Such an approach "shifts the focus of an enterprise from the sales of what it produces, to the production of what will sell" and "the philosophy of marketing dictates the social and physical production of what will sell" (1992: p. 39). His concern is the manner in which places are being constructed in the image of tourism and he notes that in the social sphere, host–guest relations are simulated through public sector training programmes (such as Welcome Host) and physically, substance is given to the promotional imagery of destinations. This commercially motivated representation of place depicts a philosophical shift from historical representation to fictional depiction. This analysis, I suggest could be extended to include events such as highland games, which are proliferating throughout Scotland in an attempt to attract and satisfy the perceived needs of the tourist, albeit orchestrated at a more local level.

Referring to tourism in the developing world, Mowforth and Munt (1998) usefully summarise shifts in contemporary tourism by making distinctions between old and new tourism and thereby providing a profile of the postmodern tourist (see Figure 1).

Although Scotland was one of the first countries to be visited by early package tourists, it did not retain this lead. While there is certainly evidence of 'mass' tourism in Scotland, such as Butlins and coach tours the majority of tourists are independent travellers and this has probably always been the case. The true rise of the package holiday as it is now known, came about after the Second World War when air transport enabled the development of the Mediterranean resorts. During this time, Scotland witnessed an era known as the Open Road, when railways gave way to coach tours and private cars. Scotland's environment and society, which have always featured strongly

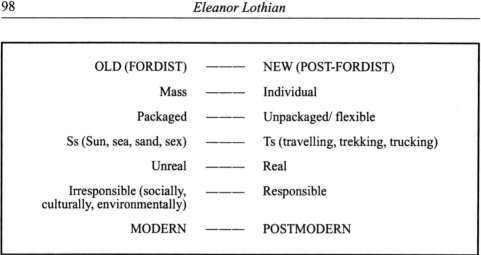

Figure 1   *'Old' tourism compared to 'new' tourism*
               (Source: Mowforth and Munt, 1998)

in the tourism product, have pulled through, with some exceptions, relatively unscathed, posing the question that responsible tourism has, more or less, always been a feature of Scottish tourism. While the contemporary visitor to Scotland may not be here to travel, trek and truck (although there is an emerging backpacker market), broadly speaking, they are here to enjoy substitute Ts, including culture and heritage, the environment and activities such as golf.

The consumption of cultural heritage by tourists is by no means a new phenomenon to Scotland. As Urry points out, "much tourism has also been minimally modernist" and "many tourist practices, even in the past, prefigure some of the postmodern characteristics". (1990: p. 87–88). He notes that the consumption of the "romantic gaze" by early tourists was likely to have been appreciated through representations (such as photographs and literature) rather than reality. The early tourists to Scotland tended to be well educated and tutored to appreciate the wilderness and the ideal of the noble savage through the paintings of Landseer and the fiction of Scott.

While tourism may be seen as an industry, at destination level it is a product that is developed, managed, marketed and consumed. Contemporary heritage, McCrone points out, "is an 'industry' insofar as it has a product (or products), a manufacturing process, markets and consumers" (1995: p. 73). Browne provides and example of this when discussing the role of heritage in Ireland's tourism recovery, he outlines investment in product development (1994). Destinations compete for tourist spending in fiercely competitive markets, where in most cases, supply outstrips demand. Hall notes that in the postmodern society that "the commercialisation of leisure has meant that tourism is often treated as a commodity to be sold through the established rules of marketing" (1994: p. 188). Before products are developed, markets are assessed to determine if the product will be viable. In Scotland, this is evident at both national and local levels through the Scottish Tourist Board's selection of Germany, France and the USA as prime markets (STB, undated) and the Scottish Executive's move towards prioritised niche marketing (Scottish Executive: 2000). Locally, developers seeking public sector funding to build a visitor attraction must estimate visitor numbers at an early stage. In today's leisure tourism market, the power of the market and the consumer is encapsulated by a statement by Derek Reid, the former Chief Executive of the Scottish Tourist Board, that "We have to give customers what they want, not what we think they want" (quoted in *Dundee Courier*, 7 August, 1995: p. 10).

The fifth era

Hall (1991), referring to hallmark events finds that they are the image makers of modern tourism and that short-term staged attractions or hallmark events have been a primary means by which to place or keep tourism destinations on the tourist map. The use of events is widespread in tourism in Scotland and include urban events such as the long-running Edinburgh International Festival, more recently established Edinburgh Science Festival and the reimaging of Glasgow through an events strategy. Urban events have enjoyed a higher profile in Scotland and this may be partly responsible for the geographical concentration of visitors in Scotland. In America. the importance of rural festivals in community reimaging and their "important role in generating a visitor industry for their host communities" has been observed (Janiskee and Drews, 1998: p. 158). Getz (1991) finds events have an important role in destination development. They contribute to destination attractiveness; expand the tourist season; spread tourism geographically; animate sites and have an important role to play with the image of a destination. Events, if properly managed can also contribute to alternative tourism, as they can bridge the host–guest gulf, increase tourism without physical development and foster community- based tourism.

The number of games and gatherings being staged in Scotland has increased considerably over the years. For example, those affiliated to the Scottish Games Association (approximately half the games staged in Scotland in any given year) increased by around 50% between 1970–1980 (Scottish Games Association Year Books 1970 and 2000) and they continue to increase (Scottish Games Association Year Book):

Year	No. games (held in Scotland) listed in SGA yearbook
1950	33
1960	30
1970	28
1980	56
1990	63
2000	64

In 2000, 14 highland games took place in Tayside. Of these, 6 have been either revived from the inter-war years or started since around 1973 and another underwent major changes during the mid 1980s. The question here is to determine the extent that these games have been created to attract tourists to the area.

The games concerned, together with the dates recalled by those interviewed are:

Arbroath Highland Games	started 1985
The Atholl Gathering and Highland Games	revived in 1983
Blairgowrie Highland Games	rejuvenated 1985
Forfar Highland Games	revived 1975
Kenmore Highland Games	revived 1970s
Montrose	revived 1978
Perth Highland Games	revived 1977

Tourism was stated to be the main reason for this at all but two games, these being Perth and Forfar (interviews, Tayside, March 1998). There can be little doubt that the remaining five games were revived for tourism benefits although other community benefits may also be apparent. A fifth era from 1970 onwards is therefore, tentatively, discernible.

Additional evidence to support this is the involvement of local authorities in organising games. In Grampian, the local authorities administer the games held in Aberdeen and Stonehaven. Dundee City Council was responsible for the Dundee Highland Games from the early 1970s to 1993 and ran the Games as part of the Come to Dundee campaign. Stirling Tourist Association is one of the main sponsors of Stirling Highland Games and attracting tourists is one of the main reasons for this involvement.

A further development during the 1980s was the emergence of, what can be termed "commercial" games. These games are not run by the community, instead, they are run by outsiders for commercial gains and they, without doubt, run for tourists. The first appears to have taken place in 1985 at the present site of Rothiemurcus Games and were called the Aviemore Highland Games. The following year, the operator lost the site to the newly founded International Federation of Heavy Events Athletes (IFHEA). In conjunction with the late Duke of Atholl, the IFHEA founded the Blair Atholl Games, which are held in front of the castle and timed to coincide with the Atholl Highlanders" Gathering. In 1987 the operator of the original Aviemore Highland Games organised a circuit of Games round the north-east of Scotland in areas where games did not exist at that time (although Games may have taken place previously in these locations), such as Nairn, Fochabers and Inverness. The Games however, did not prove to be commercially successful and the operator ceased to run them in 1993.

Commercial games were also staged in Edinburgh from 1996. These games were instigated in response to market research that revealed that tourists (German, Italian and English) were looking for highland games. In 1998, the games had been adapted to include an International Strongman Event as well as the traditional events and were being staged fortnightly (interview, March 1998). A common characteristic is that all these games take place in established tourist areas. The Blair Atholl Games in Perthshire for example, are staged next to Tayside's busiest tourist route, the A9.

It is possible therefore to categorise contemporary Highland games in the following manner:

- *Traditional Games* — established either before or during the reign of Queen Victoria and where there is evidence of the folk origins (pre 1745) in the programme of events. No further activities are offered on the field. An example of this would be Glenisla.
- *Modern Games* — established during the same era but the programme of activities has expanded to include non-traditional events. An example of this is the Strathardle Gathering which includes a local agricultural show, funfair and musical cars.
- *Community Tourism Games* — established or re-established since 1970, instigated by members of the local community with one of the objectives being to provide an event to attract tourists. Blairgowrie, Killin, Montrose and Arbroath fit this category. Games which partly fit this category but are not run for tourism purposes, such as those held in Perth and Forfar, could be regarded as Community games.
- *Commercial Tourism Games* — established or re-established since 1985 in tourist areas. Organised by a commercial operator who is most likely not to be a member of the community. The Atholl Gathering and Highland Games are an example of this.

Commodification of tradition

In today's competitive tourism markets, events are now seen to be critical in managing the image of a destination and, in turn, destination image is an important determinant of tourist buying behaviour. Butler and Hall note that images and myths "are powerful things and it is these that advertisers sell" (1998: p. 121). Dewailly recommends that for the tourist "it is important to identify destinations by a simple, even simplistic, image of a heritage" (1998: p. 127). Morgan and Prichard see the need to develop brands to "shout above the crowd" because in today's communication-saturated society, it is imperative to create a unique product image in the consumers" mind (1998: p. 141). This seems somewhat at odds with the current promotional literature of the Scottish Tourist Board, whose brochures depict scenery of Scotland that could be confused with Ireland, Wales or Scandinavia, who are ironically, close competitors. Even more ironic is that the visual image of highland games is world wide, probably one of the most instantly recognised and attributed icons. Put simply, in terms of developing a brand, Scotland has a long established and unique image, for although they may have tenuous links with their true historical roots, in terms of tourism imagery, highland games have been shouting (loudly) above the crowd for almost two centuries. A remarkable feat but perhaps more remarkable is the fact that it appears no longer to be relevant in imaging Scotland. This may partly explain the state of rural tourism in Scotland.

Getz recognises that tourist events are "consciously developed and promoted as tourist attractions" but that there is a risk that "tourism might destroy cultural authenticity, the very thing contemporary travellers appear to be seeking" (1994: p. 313). The highland games that we know are not authentic, they were largely created in the nineteenth century, yet they play an important role in Scottish identity. Highland dress was made fashionable by Sir Walter Scott and highland games were instigated mainly by landowners and given a royal seal of approval by Queen Victoria. If we are to believe Mowforth and Munt (1998), the postmodern tourist is searching for the authentic. Tourists at highland games will see a colourful spectacle that has tenuous links to the past that it is supposed to resemble. However, games can be seen to legitimise the selection of traditions and sometimes provide meanings to customs and practices that serve to distort history. The following extract from the "Glenisla Program" (1996) is intended to provide visitors with an insight to the meaning of the dance Seann Truibhas.

SEANN TRUIBHAS
This is a graceful dance, in Gaelic meaning "old trousers", which starts slowly and increases in tempo in the final two steps. This dance recognised the repression under the Jacobite Rebellion of 1745 when both Bagpipes and Kilt were banned. Any dancing had to be done in trousers and the slow tempo represents the disgust at having to do so whilst the shaking movements represent the shaking off of the trews and the quick steps are a display of pleasure when the Scots were once more able to wear the kilt.

This explanation is somewhat at odds with both Jarvie (1991) and Trevor Roper (1984) who both note that the working Scots were reluctant to return to the kilt. Referring to tartan and bagpipes, Jarvie (1991: p. 46) writes:

At the level of popular culture there is little evidence to suggest that clansfolk ever resumed the practice. For them such cultural artefacts belonged to the old tradition, a way of life that been largely destroyed during the second half of the eighteenth century. By the time Sir Walter Scott had published Waverly in

1814, the history of the Highlander had already begun to be not only distorted, but romanticised.

Trevor-Roper (1984: p. 24) states:

After a generation in trousers, the simple peasantry of the Highlands saw no reason to resume the belted plaid or the tartan which they had once found so cheap and serviceable. They did not even turn to the "handy and convenient" new kilt.

Getz makes it clear that events which have historical themes, should, by definition "embody high levels of authenticity" and that events should provide interpretation of the past by (amongst others), revealing meanings such as values and traditions, revealing interrelationships such as between social and cultural groups" and "are authentic in reflecting community values and accurately portraying historic events or objects" (1994: pp. 331–332). Highland games, in one sense, fail to satisfy these expectations. They extend Scott's 19th century deception of unity by giving today's tourists the impression that the relationship between the landowner and the working people is as it was before 1745. They do little to inform curious twenty first century visitors about the clearances and their link to contemporary landownership; surely more relevant to cultural understanding and probably more interesting than watching a trouser dance. From this, it can be derived that the games are staged, as, in the spirit of Goffman (1959), there is an arena for performances, space for spectators and an area for trading stalls. Furthermore, they conform with McCannell (1976), as there are outward signs of an important social redefinition of the categories 'truth' and 'reality' taking place.

On the other hand, it is easy to revel in historical deficiencies at the expense of failing to understand the perspective of hard pressed local tourism operators. Perhaps they are more aware that "commerce and culture are indissolubly linked in the postmodern" (Urry, 1990: p. 85). It should also be taken into account that many traditional and modern highland games, in broadly their current form, have been running for almost two centuries, a noteworthy historical achievement by many standards. Tourism games can be seen as a late twentieth century episode in the ongoing games phenomenon.

However, in the case of the Commercial Games, concern is being expressed that these games are staging non-traditional spectacles to attract tourists. Fraser (1999: p. 10), writing in *Scotland on Sunday,* notes significant departures from the traditional events at the new Aviemore and Spey Valley gathering, where bagpipes will compete with motorbikes in an effort to attract spectators to the arena. These new games were blamed for the collapse of the more traditional Rothiemurchus games and are described by the Scottish Games Association as "Renegade Games".

Conclusion

There can be little doubt that Highland Games are being staged for tourist consumption. Building on Jarvie's four era model, these games do indeed appear to signify a fifth era. Highland games have proliferated throughout Scotland since around 1970 and in Tayside, it was found that this had been done to help local tourism development and for commercial gain. In both rural and urban Scotland, games are being organised by local communities in response to a downturn in tourism and by commercial operators in established tourist areas. Four types of games become apparent: traditional, modern, community tourism and commercial tourism.

The issue of authenticity is not strictly relevant because despite many claiming pre-Jacobite connections, they are largely a product of the 19th century and most have limited associations with this earlier era. However, the selection of and commodification of tradition is much more relevant. Important elements of Scottish history that are not so readily available may result in tourists leaving with a distorted impression of both historical and contemporary Scotland and of those selected traditions which are commodified for tourism.

Acknowledgements

The author would like to acknowledge the assistance received from Mr Ian Robb, undergraduate student on the BA (Hons) Tourism programme at the University of Abertay Dundee.

References

Browne, S. (1994) 'Heritage in Ireland's tourism recovery', in M. J. Fladmark (ed) *Cultural tourism*. London: Donhead Publishing Ltd.

Butler, R. C. and Hall, C. M. (1998) 'Image and reimaging of rural areas' in R. C. Butler, C. M. Hall and J. Jenkins (eds) *Tourism and recreation in rural areas*. Chichester: Wiley.

Dewailly, M. (1998) 'Image and reimaging of rural areas', in R. C. Butler, C. M. Hall and J. Jenkins (eds) *Tourism and recreation in rural areas*. Chichester: Wiley.

Fraser, S. (1999) 'Wheelie of fortune comes to the games', *Scotland on Sunday* (Edinburgh: The Scotsman Publications Ltd): June 27: p. 10.

Getz, D. (1991) *Festivals, special events and tourism*. New York: Van Nostrand Reinhold.

—— (1994) 'Event tourism and the authenticity dilemma', in W. Theobald (ed) *Global tourism: The next decade*. Oxford: Butterworth-Heinemann.

—— (1997) *Event management and event tourism*. New York: Cognizant Communications Corporation.

Goffman, E. (1959) *The presentation of self in everyday life*. New York: Doubleday.

Gold, J. R. and Gold, M. M. (1995) *Imagining Scotland: Tradition, representation and promotion in Scottish tourism since 1750*. Alershot: Scolar.

Gray, A. (2000) '£100m lost to Scots economy as visitors stay away', *The Scotsman* (Edinburgh: The Scotsman Publications Ltd.) July 7: p. 1.

Hall, C. M. (1991) *Hallmark tourist events: Impacts, management and planning*. London: Belhaven.

Hall, C. M. (1994) *Tourism and politics: Policy, power, place*. Chichester: Wiley.

Hughes, G. (1992) 'Tourism and the grographical imagination', *Leisure Studies* Vol. 11, No. 1: pp. 31–42.

Janiskee, R. L. and Drews, P. L. (1998) 'Rural festivals and community reimaging', in R. C. Butler, C. M. Hall and J. Jenkins (eds) *Tourism and recreation in rural areas*. Chichester: Wiley.

Jarvie, G. (1991) *The Highland Games: The making of the myth*. Edinburgh: Edinburgh University Press.

—— (1999) *Sport in the making of Celtic cultures*. London: Leicester University Press.

Jarvie, G. and Walker, G. (1994) *Scottish sport in the making of a nation*. London: Leicester University Press.

McCannell, D. (1976) *The tourist: A new theory of the leisure class*. London: Macmillan.

McCrone, D. (1995) *Scotland the brand*. Edinburgh: Edinburgh University Press.

Morgan, N. and Prichard, A. (1998) *Tourism promotion and power: Creating images, creating identities*. Chichester: Wiley.

Morton, T. (2000) 'No place like home?', *The Scotsman* (Edinburgh: The Scotsman Publications Ltd.): 10 July: p. 4.

Mowforth, M., and Munt, I. (1998) *Tourism and sustainability: New tourism in the third world*. London: Routledge.

Scottish Executive (2000) *A New Strategy for Scottish Tourism*. Edinburgh: The Stationery Bookshop.

Scottish Games Association (1950; 1970; 2000) *Annual Year Book*. Publisher unknown.

—— (1960) *Annual Year Book*. Stirling: Learmonth.

—— (1980) *Annual Year Book*. Renfrew: Gardner Gibson Print Limited.

—— (1985) *Annual Year Book*. Arbroath: The Herald Press.

—— (1990) *Annual Year Book*. Perth: McKinlay.

Scottish Tourist Board (undated) *International Marketing Plan 1997/98*. Edinburgh: Scottish Tourist Board.

————— (1998) *Strategic Plan Progress Report*. Edinburgh: Scottish Tourist Board.

————— (1999) *Strategic Plan Interim Review*. Edinburgh: Scottish Tourist Board.

Seaton, A. V. and Hay, B. (1998) 'The marketing of Scotland as a tourist destination, 1985–96', in R. MacLellan and R. Smith (eds) *Tourism in Scotland*. London: International Thomson Press.

Tayside Economic Research Centre (1999) *Annual Report*. Dundee: University of Abertay Dundee.

Trevor-Roper, H. (1984) 'Invention of tradition: The Highland tradition of Scotland', in E. Hobsbawm and T. Ranger (eds) *The invention of tradition*. Cambridge: Cambridge University Press.

Urry, J. (1990) *The tourist gaze: Leisure and travel in contemporary societies*. London: Sage.

Leaflets and Brochures

Blairgowrie Highland Games (1998) *Blairgowrie Highland Games Programme*. Publisher unknown.

Glenisla Highland Games (1996) *Glenisla Highland Games and Gathering Program*. Publisher unknown.

Scottish Enterprise Tayside (2000) *Tayside Tourism Statistics*. Dundee: Scottish Enterprise Tayside.

Scottish Tourist Board (1997) *Scotland Where to go and What to See*. Edinburgh: Scottish Tourist Board.

Scottish Tourist Board (undated). *Scotland Your Essential Guide 2000*. Edinburgh: Scottish Tourist Board.

Web sites

http://www.holiday.scotland.net/seeanddo/index.htm   www   .holiday.scotland.net/ seeanddo/index.htm

www.staruk.org.uk

Haggis and Heritage — Representing Scotland in the United States

Euan Hague

Geography Department, Syracuse University, New York

Introduction

US interest in Scottish heritage has grown considerably since the late 1960s to the point of becoming an "obsession" (Hunter, 1997: p. 17). The US Navy, Air Force, Marine Corps and Military Academy have all registered their own 'official' tartans, as have eighteen states (Hewitson, 1993; Young and Macfarlane, 1998). Numerous clan societies, genealogical organisations, magazines, newspapers and bagpipe bands have been founded to meet demand within the Scottish-American community[1]. Further, such is the popularity of Scotland in the United States that in 1998 the Senate declared 6 April to be annually celebrated as 'National Tartan Day' (Congressional Record: Senate, 1998; Linklater, 1998).

The most visible aspects of this growing US interest in Scottish heritage are Highland Games and Scottish festivals[2]. In 1979 there were sixty such events in the United States (Berthoff, 1982). By the early 1990s, between seventy-five and a hundred Scottish heritage events occurred annually (Brander, 1992; 1996). At the end of the twentieth century, depending on your source, there are between two and three hundred Scottish games and festivals (Ray, 1998; Roberts, 1999a; Cornwell, 2000). Such is the popularity of Scottish heritage in the US that Fry (1998: p. 19) confidently asserts, "there is not one of the 50 states that does not host some sort of Scottish celebrations every year".

Due to their being the most visible manifestations of Scottish heritage in the United States, this paper examines the development and role of Scottish festivals and Highland Games. My study is divided into three main sections. Initially, I outline the spatial and temporal expansion of such events. The second empirical section draws on comments made by members of the Scottish-American community in a north-eastern US state whom I interviewed in 1997–1998. The third section assesses recent writing about Highland Games, primarily focusing on events held in some Southern US states. Each of these sections utilises different data and they should be understood in parallel as separate analyses of Highland Games and Scottish festivals in the United States, and also combined to build a composite assessment of the development of such events and their standing at the turn of the twenty-first century.

Analysing Highland Games and Scottish festivals in Scotland, Jarvie (1991) sets his examination within the context of Highland development and Scottish historical processes. Further, Jarvie (1991: p. 2) demands that an assessment of Highland Games as "cultural form[s]" must be set within wider sociological understandings and theoretical underpinnings. Arguing that context is "absolutely crucial" to examining events such as Highland Games, Jarvie's subsequent work situates Highland Games in nineteenth century North America within the context of contemporaneous Scottish emigration to Canada and the United States (Jarvie, 2000: p. 40). To this end, my focus on late-twentieth century Scottish heritage events in the US is located within the theoretical context regarding the production and consumption of heritage at the end of the twentieth century.

The production and consumption of heritage

Two of the major theorists of 'heritage' are Wright (1991) and Hewison (1987). Writing at the height of Thatcherism, their assessments of heritage in Britain are scathing. Wright (1991) challenges heritage processes as founded within a regressive conservative ideology that is imperialistic, nostalgic, and comprises an exclusionary and nationalistic response to a national history and identity that are perceived to be under threat. Consequently, heritage constructs a "nationalist fable", glorifying and sanitising the past, and commercially producing it for mass consumption (Wright, 1991: p. 181). Hewison's (1987) well-known critique, *The Heritage Industry*, is similarly dismissive. Paralleling Wright, Hewison (1987) contends, "the development of heritage not only involves the reassertion of values that are anti-democratic, but the heightening of decline through a stifling of the culture of the present" (Urry, 1990: p. 109). These authors thus conceptualise 'heritage' as a reactionary myth, national fiction, and a decontextualised theatrical performance of the past.

The arguments of Wright (1991) and Hewison (1987) are pertinent but not beyond challenge. Urry (1990), amongst others, has criticised these understandings for constructing heritage as a monolithic, conservative version of the past that people consume uncritically and unthinkingly accept as fact. Proposing that heritage sites and activities are often ambiguous, enabling people to add their own interpretations to those produced by the dominant heritage narrative, Urry (1990) further contends that Hewison (1987), in particular, fails to account for the popular demand for historical and environmental conservation. Ashworth (1994: p. 16) in turn, states that, "each individual necessarily determines the constitution of each unique heritage product at the moment of consumption", and thus rather than being a wistful customer of institutionally-produced mass nostalgia, the heritage consumer is an agent who decides, in each instance, on the 'authenticity' of the past which is represented.

In the context of the current study, it is important to note that state agencies are rarely involved in the production of Scottish heritage events in the United States. Rather, a majority of these are organised by local St. Andrew's Societies or Highland Games committees that are staffed by volunteers and enthusiasts who also participate in Scottish heritage events. To this end, the production of Scottish heritage in the United States contrasts with the model of institutionally produced 'heritage' outlined by Wright (1991) and Hewison (1987), and is more aligned with the understandings outlined by Urry (1990) and Ashworth (1994) who centre the role of consumers in the construction of heritage. The producers of Scottish heritage events in the United States are the same people who comprise the major consumers of these festivities. As such, there is a self-production of heritage by community members. Recognising the difference between 'self-' and 'officially-' produced heritage events, Kirshenblatt-Gimblett (1998: p. 73) observes that for ethnic festivals in the United States, those "organised by dominant cultural institutions such as museums and state folklife programs or funded by state and federal agencies share a performance discourse that often stands in contrast (if not in opposition) to the ways communities stage themselves". Differences in production of these celebrations subsequently, "offer different approaches to the marketing of authenticity" (Kirshenblatt-Gimblett, 1998: p. 73).

A discourse of 'authenticity' is a critical defining component of heritage production and consumption. Whereas Hewison (1987) and Wright (1991) dismiss heritage as a version of history that is anything but 'authentic,' Urry (1990) and Ashworth (1994) suggest consumers can make up their own minds. McCrone *et al.* (1995: p. 8) further argue that people "search for the authentic through heritage", in particular, the authenticity of the past, self and nation. Such a connection, between heritage and a quest for an 'authentic identity', has occurred at the end of the twentieth century. This time period saw "issues of identity become especially problematic" and resulted in, "a search for roots, for discovering where we have come from" (McCrone *et al.*, 1995: p. 25). The question of 'authenticity' is one faced repeatedly by members of the north-eastern Scottish-American community in which I was a participant and observer. These Scottish-Americans both host and visit Highland Games and Scottish festivals in the United States and, as I outline below, there were disagreements within this Scottish-American community as to who is 'authentically' Scottish.

A fundamental aspect of Scottish heritage in the United States is, therefore, the discovery of one's 'authentic' Scottish identity. This is typically achieved through the construction of genealogy. Many people attending Scottish heritage events have traced ancestors who were born in Scotland and, however atavistic a process, this makes a personal connection to Scotland. Intertwining a search for genealogical 'roots' and the production of 'ethnic' heritage is a common relationship in the United States (Kirshenblatt-Gimblett, 1998). At major US tourist sites like Ellis Island, which served as a processing centre for immigrants between 1892–1924, "heritage is reduced to genealogy" because visitors are only included in the heritage discourse by virtue of their ancestry (Kirshenblatt-Gimblett, 1998: p. 182). Tracing one's forebears or, perhaps more likely, imagining that one's ancestors entered the United States at Ellis Island, becomes a fundamental process of both producing and consuming heritage at this location. The role of genealogy at Scottish heritage events, as I discuss below, is somewhat similar.

Theories of 'heritage' typically recognise its production and consumption as a commercial process and that issues of 'authenticity', particularly of individual or national 'roots', are of critical importance. A further assertion in this literature is that heritage is also fundamentally about place. Ashworth (1994: p. 19), for example, envisages "a strong reciprocal link between heritage and places" and as a result, "places frequently are the heritage product". Many assessments of heritage, therefore, look at sites that have been renovated and reconstructed as tourist attractions (e.g. Wright, 1991; Hewison, 1987; Ashworth and Larkham, 1994; McCrone *et al.*, 1995). Consequently, such theorists understand 'heritage' to be produced at an identifiable location, by an identifiable author, with people subsequently visiting that museum or exhibit as heritage consumers. Thus, heritage is a phenomenon thoroughly enmeshed in global systems of tourism and economic development (Urry, 1990; McCrone *et al.*, 1995). At Scottish heritage events in the United States the place being produced is neither a representation of a local past nor former workplaces being reproduced as "exhibitions of themselves" (Kirshenblatt-Gimblett, 1998: p. 7). Rather, the heritage location depicted is a stereotypical and romantic Scotland complete with bagpipes, tartan, kilt-wearing clansmen and caber tossing competitions — a representation that developed in Scotland in the late-eighteenth and nineteenth centuries (Jarvie 1991; McCrone *et al.*, 1995). Yet, importantly, Highland Games and Scottish festivals are producing this Scotland within the United States, not in the 'authentic' location of the activities depicted, but a location in a different continent, four thousand miles away from Scotland.

"There's certainly a temptation", as a result of this distant reproduction of clichéd representations of Scotland, "to dismiss the Scottish-American scene as a superficial hotch-potch of bagpipes, caber-tossing and swirling kilts, peopled by groups of slightly eccentric enthusiasts locked in a 'loch and glen' mentality, a past which effectively vanished after Culloden [1746]" (Hewitson, 1993: p. 282). However, I contend that a more illuminating way to proceed is to interrogate the relationship between heritage, people and place at Scottish festivals and Highland Games in the United States. As the following spatial and temporal data shows, increasing numbers of people are attending Scottish heritage events in the United States where, as Roberts (1999a: p. 15) notes, they "celebrate a place, or the idea of a place, that few of them have seen".

Highland Games and Scottish Festivals in the United States

Caledonian Societies have existed in North America since the mid-eighteenth century and Highland Games since the mid-nineteenth (Berthoff, 1982; Donaldson, 1986; Jarvie, 1991, 2000). Despite this longevity it is difficult to get a precise picture of how many Scottish Games and festivals are currently held in the USA. Some events are long-standing and have been held annually since the nineteenth century, others have lapsed and restarted, while still more are only a year old or were proposed for inauguration in 2000. To gain an accurate picture of the distribution of Highland Games and Scottish festivals in the United States, I utilised six different sources that provide lists of on-going Scottish heritage events: Donaldson (1986), Brander (1992; 1996), US Scots (1996), and two internet directories (Internet 1997; 2000). These sources identified a growth from seventy-five annual events in 1986 to two hundred and five planned for 2000 (Table 1). After building a database from these sources, I assessed them for spatial, temporal and spatio-temporal descriptions of Scottish heritage events in the United States.

Table 1:   Total number of annual Highland Games and Scottish Festivals in the
               United States listed by each data source.

Data Source	Date of publication	Number of Highland Games and Scottish Festivals listed
Donaldson	1986	75
Brander	1992	100
Brander	1996	74
US Scots	1996	162
Internet	1997	148
Internet	2000	205
Composite Data Set	1986–2000	128

Spatial distribution by state

From each source I identified the number of Highland Games and Scottish festivals in each US state. What was immediately noticeable is that increasing numbers of US states inaugurated Scottish heritage festivals in the final years of the Twentieth Century. Whereas in the mid-1980s many states, particularly in the mid-west such as Kansas, Nebraska, the Dakotas and Iowa, did not host Scottish festivals (Donaldson, 1986), by 2000 only Wyoming, North Dakota and Delaware remained as states where, according to available data, Scottish heritage events are not taking place (Internet 2000; see Table 2). Between 1986 and 2000, a gradual 'filling in' of the United States occurred with more and more areas deciding to inaugurate Scottish festivals. It is interesting to note that the

Table 2: *Highland Games and Scottish Festivals per US state: 1986 and 2000*

State	No. of Highland Games and Scottish Festivals in the United States in 1986 (n=75) Source: Donaldson (1986)	No. of Highland Games and Scottish Festivals in the United States in 2000 (n=205) Source: Internet (2000)
Alabama	1	3
Alaska	1	1
Arizona	1	3
Arkansas	1	3
California	11	27
Colorado	5	7
Connecticut	2	3
Delaware	0	0
Florida	3	11
Georgia	3	5
Hawaii	1	1
Idaho	0	1
Illinois	1	4
Indiana	0	3
Iowa	0	2
Kansas	0	4
Kentucky	0	3
Louisiana	0	2
Maine	2	2
Maryland	2	8
Massachusetts	1	3
Michigan	2	4
Minnesota	1	2
Mississippi	0	3
Missouri	2	3
Montana	0	3
Nebraska	0	1
Nevada	0	2
New Hampshire	1	2
New Jersey	0	3
New Mexico	0	1
New York	5	11
North Carolina	3	6
North Dakota	0	0
Ohio	1	7
Oklahoma	1	3
Oregon	2	8
Pennsylvania	3	6
Rhode Island	0	2
South Carolina	1	1
South Dakota	0	2
Tennessee	1	4
Texas	5	16
Utah	2	2
Vermont	2	1
Virginia	3	7
Washington	5	7
West Virginia	0	1
Wisconsin	0	1
Wyoming	0	0
Total USA	75	205

most distant US states, namely Alaska and Hawaii, have hosted Highland Games annually since 1981 and 1982 respectively. Also these sources indicate that the four most populous states in the US — California, New York, Florida and Texas — appear strongly as the states hosting the most Scottish festivities between 1986–2000 (US Census, 2000).

Across the six data sources, the names, locations and foundation dates of Scottish Games were inconsistent. Consequently, I generated a composite data set that could be considered more reliable. Assessing detailed information about when and where events were held and which organisation was in charge of hosting them, the composite data set listed events described by three or more of the original sources (i.e. Donaldson, 1986; Brander, 1992, 1996; US Scots, 1996; Internet 1997, 2000). Where there were discrepancies, the information pertaining to a majority of data sources was taken as most probable. The picture of Scottish festivities in the United States built from this composite data set identified one hundred and twenty-eight Highland Games and Scottish festivals regularly held in the United States by 1996. Again, the dominance of California was apparent, with other states such as Texas, Maryland, New York, Virginia and Washington annually hosting six or more Scottish heritage events.

This description of where Scottish Festivals and Highland Games occur in the United States provides strong evidence of the growing popularity of such events. It also suggests that although there are regional concentrations, nearly every state now has at least one or two Scottish festivals. Having described the spatial distribution of Scottish events, I now turn to their chronology.

Temporal distribution by inauguration date

The temporal distribution was assessed in the same manner as the spatial, namely by utilising six sources and combining them into a composite data set. To evaluate the chronological development of Highland Games and Scottish festivals I plotted the inauguration dates of Scottish heritage events against a timescale and assessed the number of events inaugurated each decade and the cumulative number of Scottish heritage events in the USA[3]. This analysis identified two main trends. Firstly, there has been a substantial growth in Scottish heritage festivals at the end of the twentieth century that shows little sign of abating. This is emphasised by the correspondence between each individual data source when observing the trend in the cumulative number of Scottish heritage events (see Figure 1, page following).

Secondly, data sources suggest that a considerable proportion of this growth in the number of Scottish heritage events has occurred in the 1990s[4]. To examine this 1990s growth in more detail, data from Internet (2000), the only source to cover the entire decade, was plotted to indicate the number of Scottish heritage events inaugurated in the decade in relation to the 1980s (Figure 2, page following). Here, a clear peak of twenty new events is evident in 1996. Indeed, in the first half of the 1990s, on average five new events were started per year. In contrast, between 1995–1999 on average of

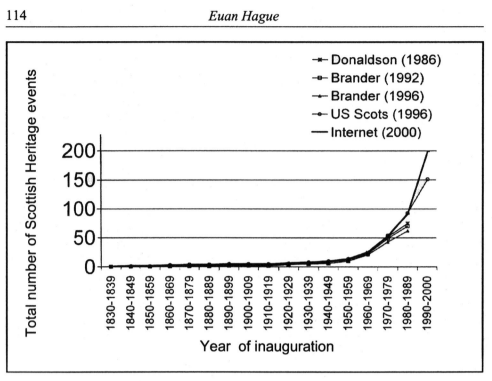

Figure 1   *Growth of Scottish Festivals and Highland Games in the US*

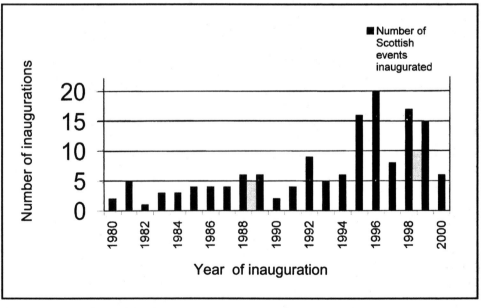

Figure 2   *Scottish Heritage events inaugurated in the USA since 1980*
                (Source: Internet, 2000)

fifteen new events per year were initiated. These last five years of the twentieth century thus saw a surge in what had been a steady trend for the previous thirty years, namely a growing interest and participation in Scottish heritage events in the United States. I suggest that a major reason for this was in reaction to the Oscar-winning film *Braveheart*. Released in 1995, this film is about Scottish medieval hero William Wallace and starred Mel Gibson. It was extremely popular in the US and spurred much interest in Scotland amongst its audience (see Hague, 2000).

Spatio-temporal distribution

Berthoff's (1982: p. 5) investigation of Scottish heritage events in the 1970s distinguished between Highland Games in the northern and mid-western US States, "where the great majority of ... Scottish immigrants ... settled" and those in the southern states. He comments that in the second half of the nineteenth century only eleven Highland Games were located in the South and that these were held irregularly. A century later there has been a significant shift. Despite few new Scottish immigrants arriving in the United States, the 1970s saw "the whole center of gravity of Scottish-America ... swinging south and west", away from the established core areas of Scottish settlement in states like New York, Wisconsin and Michigan (Berthoff, 1982: p. 14). Subsequently, "half of all Scottish-American societies base their associations in the South and more than one-third of over two hundred annual Highland games/Scottish festivals occur in the region" (Ray, 1998: p. 28).

The initial spatial assessment suggested a growing number of Scottish heritage events across the United States as a whole, whereas the temporal analysis showed there has been a large number of Scottish heritage events inaugurated at the end of the twentieth century. The longest continuously running Highland Games in the USA has been held Detroit, Michigan since 1849 (US Scots, 1996; Internet, 2000)[5]. Other long-established games include the Annual Scottish Gathering and Games hosted by the Caledonian Club of San Francisco since 1866 and the Sacramento Valley Scottish Games and Gathering began in 1876.

Based on the composite data series, Figure 3 (following page) shows three 'waves' of inauguration, providing evidence that there has been a spatial diffusion of Scottish heritage events. Before 1950, a few core areas of Scottish festivals and Highland Games existed in New York, California, Oregon, Wisconsin and Michigan. These are areas long-associated with migration from Scotland. A second wave of inauguration, between 1950–1979 saw events begin down the eastern seaboard to the southern states of Florida, Georgia and the Carolinas, and appear in western states such as Texas, Utah and Arizona. The third period, since 1980, has seen Scottish events start throughout the states along the Mississippi River, reaching Alabama, Mississippi and Louisiana, spreading across the mid-west into Montana and beyond to Alaska and Hawaii. In New Jersey and Massachusetts there were Scottish festivals in the nineteenth century but these events

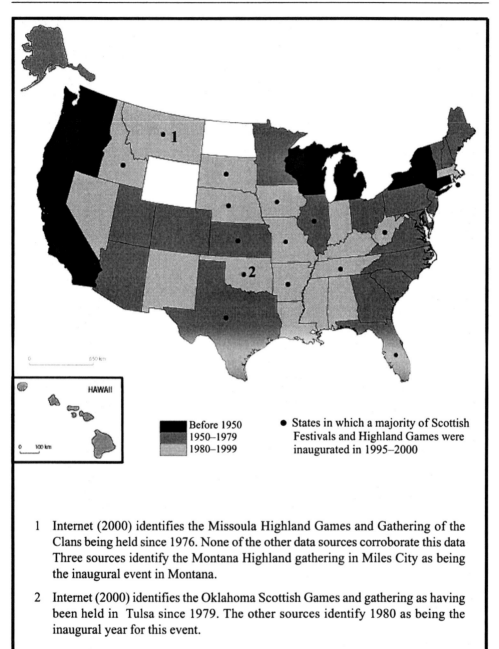

Before 1950
1950–1979
1980–1999

● States in which a majority of Scottish
Festivals and Highland Games were
inaugurated in 1995–2000

1   Internet (2000) identifies the Missoula Highland Games and Gathering of the
    Clans being held since 1976. None of the other data sources corroborate this data
    Three sources identify the Montana Highland gathering in Miles City as being
    the inaugural event in Montana.

2   Internet (2000) identifies the Oklahoma Scottish Games and gathering as having
    been held in Tulsa since 1979. The other sources identify 1980 as being the
    inaugural year for this event.

*Figure 3   Inauguration date of oldest Scottish heritage event in each state
                 (source: composite data set; Internet, 2000)*

had ceased and new events were inaugurated in 1973 and 1981 respectively (Donaldson, 1986; Jarvie 1991; Internet 2000).

Amalgamating these six data sets into a single composite, however, privileges longer-established Highland Games and Scottish festivals. Events inaugurated in the 1990s, and particularly those beginning since 1995, have less likelihood of appearing in three of these chronologically spaced data sources. As above, to highlight this discrepancy and provide a better chronological balance to the evidence presented, I utilised the most recent and comprehensive source available, that from Clan MacLachlan (Internet, 2000). Consequently, Figure 3 also shows states where more than half of all Highland Games and Scottish festivals were inaugurated since 1995. I chose 1995 as the temporal data suggested a quantitative difference between the two halves of the 1990s. The first half carried on the trend of the 1980s, namely a few inaugurations per year, but the post-*Braveheart* years saw a surge of new events. Two things are noticeable from this data. Firstly, states like California, New York, and Oregon, although having some new events beginning since 1995, have existing and well-established Scottish heritage festivals, meaning newer events remain a minority. Secondly, the major sweep of new events is across Plains states like Iowa, Kansas, Nebraska and South Dakota. These are areas that had few, if any, Scottish festivals in the past and thus there was room for growth in the late-1990s.

This section has described the general spread and distribution of Scottish festivals and Highland Games in the United States. Over the past century, the number of events has grown rapidly, in particular since the 1970s (see Figure 1). The spatial distribution of Scottish heritage events has seen populous states like California and Texas continue to host the most games. A spatial diffusion of events into southern and mid-western states since the 1980s was also noted, with places like South Dakota and Nebraska initiating their first Scottish heritage events at the end of the 1990s.

Scotland and genealogy: Discourses of 'authenticity' at Scottish heritage events in the United States

The second empirical analysis builds upon interviews I conducted in 1997–98 with members of a Scottish-American community in a north-eastern US State and focuses on issues of 'authenticity' and genealogy within this Scottish-American community[6]. Indeed, the pertinence of genealogy to Scottish heritage events in the USA cannot be under-stated. In 1982, Rowland Berthoff identified Highland Games in southern states as celebrations of genealogy with around ten times as many clan societies attending Scottish festivals and Highland Games in the south as attended such events in the north. Scottish heritage events in northern states, he explained, were primarily musical, dancing and athletic competitions (Berthoff, 1982). Interest in genealogy across the United States has grown markedly since Berthoff's study. By the 1990s, eighty percent of Scottish heritage events in the United States offered genealogical services (ASGF, 1995). Recent data reaffirms a concentration of genealogical clan societies exhibiting at events in southern states (Internet, 2000). The festival that is attended by the most clan societies (180) is Grandfather Mountain Highland Games in North Carolina. Other large representations are seen at the long-established Californian events, namely Sacramento Valley and San Francisco (100 and 75 clan societies respectively), and again in North Carolina at Loch Norman Highland Games (83 clans). At Stone Mountain, Georgia there are seventy-five clans while the largest representation in the north is at Loon Mountain, New Hampshire with seventy in attendance (Internet, 2000).

At the Highland Games in the north-eastern US state where I undertook research around twenty-five clan and genealogical organizations attend annually. One interviewee, bagpiper Kevin McCaskey, explained that a major reason for people to attend Scottish events is to discover their genealogy and, thereafter, tartan:

> To be honest, no-one's really interested in Scotland ... At the games people come up and ask "What tartan am I?" That's all they're interested in ... [and] as we don't help people to find their relatives, and that's what they want, people lose interest and go elsewhere. Most people head to the clan tents to find tartans. They go to the Games to see kilts and hear bagpipes. They only want to know what kilt they can wear and don't really care about the dancing and are often surprised to see the heavy athletics.

Clan societies and associations set up display tents and invite people with specific surnames to join their organisations (see Figure 4). There is considerable discussion within the wider Scottish-American community as to what genealogical criteria are necessary for membership and, as Berthoff (1982: p. 20) comments, "Hazy as the exact relationship may be, joining a clan association can convey satisfactions far beyond personal genealogy". Kevin McCaskey told me he had chosen to join a clan society. Although disappointed that its genealogical resources did not assist his personal investigations, Kevin explained that some clan societies are stricter on genealogical matters than others:

> I kind of joined the McCaskeys because of the genealogy thing. They advertised that they had a genealogical library ... but the library really wasn't very good regarding specific genealogical data, although it had good general information about Scottish clans and history ... On the forms to join they asked roughly if you were related to the McCaskeys, but all you had to do was sketch a list showing the connection, you didn't have to prove it and I suppose you could make it up. Some societies anyone can join if they are interested in Scotland and clan history, but others are more strict and you have to be Scottish. Some hereditary societies are very strict ... you have to provide proofs like birth and death certificates. By comparison, joining the McCaskeys was easy.

Figure 4   *Clan MacNeil Association of America display tent (right: detail)*
at a northeastern US state Highland Games, 1997

The centrality of genealogy to some members of this north-eastern US state's Scottish-American community does not, however, go uncontested. Unlike US-born participants such as Kevin McCaskey, those born in Scotland rarely play bagpipes or join clan societies. In many instances, an initial enthusiasm for participating in Scottish heritage activities in the USA fades. Don Campbell left Scotland in 1952, initially participating in Highland Games in this north-eastern state as a drummer in a pipe band however, "after a couple of years" he gave up because, "it got to be too much in the end, getting dressed up and hauling that drum everywhere". Since he finished drumming, Don Campbell explained, "I have no real connection with any Scottish affairs except the annual Games. I have gone to the Games in the past, but it conflicts with the annual member and guest tournament at the golf club". Today, Don Campbell prefers to play golf than attend the annual Highland Games in his locale, an event that regularly attracts over four thousand visitors. When I asked him, 'Who are the people involved with Scottish events in this area?' his answer was revealing:

There is not really a big Scottish contingent here … Some of those involved
here do have a Scottish background but in general *they are all Americans*. I
used to work in the beer tent with [a man] who lives here and he's Scottish, but
I can't think of anyone else. Most of those involved enjoy the thrill of being
associated with the pipes and drums. No, I can't think of anyone who has *a real
tie back to Scotland*. (my emphasis)

Paul Martin made a similar observation about the participants in Scottish heritage events
in the United States. Born in England, Paul Martin became involved with Highland
Games because of his interest in Celtic music. He remarked, "Americans like to *pretend*
that they are Irish, German, Scottish or whatever" (my emphasis). Don Campbell and
Paul Martin, therefore, present a consensus of opinion that understands Scottish-
Americans who are born in the United States and claim their Scottishness atavistically,
not so much as inventing these ancestral connections, but certainly over-stretching them.
John Barr, another man who emigrated from Western Scotland in the 1950s, stated:

The only Scottish thing I participate in in this area is the Scottish Games [but]
I'm not really into the other things like clan societies and all that stuff, the fanatics I call them. I don't need to belong to a group like that to know that I have
a Scottish background … People can go overboard with their Scottishness here.
I call them fanatics. 99.9% of the people in the pipe band here wouldn't know
Scotland if they saw it … For example, there's a chiropractor about a mile away
from here called Robertson. He must have come here about when I did in the
1950s, but his son is the one that is the Scottish fanatic. He is in the pipe band
and wears his kilt every other weekend.

In this statement, John Barr draws a contrast between those born in Scotland, namely
himself and the chiropractor, and the "fanatics" who are active enthusiasts participating
regularly in Scottish heritage events, such as the chiropractor's son. The distinction made
is by identifying the "fanatics" as those born in the United States. A genealogical rather
than natal connection to Scotland is one that, as Paul Martin and Don Campbell also
imply, produces a somewhat tenuous Scottish identity.

   These three British-born participants in the Scottish-American community highlight
an important issue in relation to the construction of an 'authentic' Scottish identity at
heritage events in the United States. John Barr stated he did not need to be involved with
Scottish events to know of his own Scottishness, whereas Don Campbell stated that the
"Americans" involved in organising the Scottish Games in this area do not have "real
tie[s]" to Scotland. In turn, Paul Martin stated that the European ethno-nationalities
claimed by people born in the United States are "pretend". Yet if the authenticity of
heritage is, as Ashworth (1994) asserts, for a consumer to evaluate, an individual's
decision to identify their Scottish genealogy generates an 'authentic' Scottish
connection. In the following excerpt, Ian and Alice Naysmith discuss their participation
in Scottish heritage events. Two key aspects emerge. Firstly, although the mother of Ian

Naysmith's father migrated from Skye to the United States, he is the only member of his family to engage with this ancestry and join Scottish heritage organisations. Secondly, Alice Naysmith notes that Scottish heritage events generate a "sense of belonging" for the increasing number of people attending them.

> Alice Naysmith: I think that all the Scottish events in the area are getting more and more people going to them, which is good … I think that the Games community gives people a sense of belonging … The games create a tradition and without them that sense of belonging may have been lost.

> Ian Naysmith: I was the first person in my family to take an interest in Scottish groups in America. And perhaps I'll be the last … My father was not interested in the games and societies, neither is my sister. She will listen to my stories, but she won't take an active interest in Scotland.

Dorothy Kerr also sought a "sense of belonging". Another bagpiper, she decided to concentrate on tracing her Scottish ancestors despite having other forebears from a range of European countries. Noting she is "a seventh or eighth generation immigrant", Dorothy Kerr examined the reasons as to why many people born in the United States research their genealogies: "…people go back and discover their ethnic roots and then join heritage groups. These groups do to some extent manufacture that sense of belonging, be it Italian, German, Scots or Irish. They enable one to build a kind of surrogate family around us, our own family being spread far and wide across America".

In combination, Scottish heritage groups and the discovery of her "ethnic roots" generate a "sense of belonging" for Dorothy Kerr, yet she also recognises that heritage organisations play a central role in the production of this sentiment. Indeed, many of those I interviewed noted that Scottish heritage in the United States was a constructed, commercial product. Alongside the clan society displays at Scottish Games and festivals are small business vendors selling Scottish-themed products. Event organisers regularly debate whom to invite to sell their wares and the following excerpt is from a conversation between Paul and Susie Martin. Paul Martin is the Englishman quoted above. His wife, Susie, is not involved with these events, nor does she have Scottish ancestry, yet she attends Scottish festivals with her family:

> Susie: They sell the same stuff over and over. I went and looked around … the vendors were not selling anything I had not seen before. In fact there was nothing that I had not seen for the last five years.

> Paul: But other people come back year after year. The issue of vendors is the annual debate at our [Highland] Games. Do we stick with those who have supported us in the past or do we say "Thanks, but we want something new".

> Susie: But all that they do is promote a stereotype. All that they sell is the same. Look at the T-shirts we got the boys with the thistles on.

Paul: It was Robert the Bruce.

Susie: Whatever was on them, it was the same as ever. There is nothing new, there's those usual Scottish terrier dog T-shirts at every stall.

Paul: Okay, so the Games is promoting a stereotype, and a stereotype that didn't really exist before the Victorian era. The Games pays very little attention to the other stuff in Scotland and that goes on elsewhere.

Like Susie and Paul Martin, Jim Donaldson, who regularly attends Scottish festivals as a clan society member, recognises these heritage events are commercially produced representations of an imagined Scotland:

Jim Donaldson: You look at Scotland and then look at what the Highland Games sell and compare that to Scotland's popular image. Not only are these images what the Games sell, they are also what the Scottish Tourist Board sells, bagpipes, kilts and cabers.

Jim Donaldson makes it clear that he understands the representations of Scotland produced and consumed within the United States reflect those sold by the Scottish Tourist Board to audiences abroad. Thus he implies that this version of Scotland should not be dismissed as fallacious because a major source of its production is within Scotland. Rather, despite its content, the Scotland of the USA's Scottish heritage events is one that was created in Scotland, conferring upon it a sense of 'authenticity.' Throughout these testimonies it is clear that the understandings of 'heritage' by these individuals fall within both the theories proposed by Urry (1990) and Ashworth (1994), namely that heritage consumers determine the 'authenticity' of the heritage practices, and also those of Wright (1991) and Hewison (1987) which assess heritage as mass-produced representations of the past. Consequently, individuals within this Scottish-American community differently interpret issues of 'authenticity', both of Scottish events and claims to Scottish identity.

Ethnicity and 'racial' identity at Highland Games and Scottish Festivals in the United States

My third analysis of Scottish heritage events in the United States reviews recent assessments of Highland Games, much of which centres on Scottish heritage events held in Southern US states. In July 1978 *Newsweek* magazine featured an article entitled "Scotland the South" which celebrated the Highland Games held at Grandfather Mountain in North Carolina (Shah and Arthur, 1978). In many ways, "Scotland the South" is a more appropriate moniker today than it was twenty years ago. Berthoff's (1982) assessment of Scottish heritage activities in 1979 noted only seventeen Highland Games and Heritage Festivals were held in the American South compared to forty-three outside this region. Today, this spatial distribution, as the data presented above shows, has changed with the pre-eminent interest in Scottish heritage shifting from north to south.

Across the US South, however, some Scottish heritage events are held on what Roberts (1997; 1999a; 1999b) considers problematic local sites, namely former plantation estates and shrines commemorating the nineteenth century Confederate States of America. One well-known Confederate memorial is Stone Mountain, on the outskirts of Atlanta, Georgia. Here likenesses of Confederate Civil War heroes are carved into a cliff face. Since 1973 this location has been the site of a Highland Games that currently attracts twelve thousand visitors (Internet, 2000). At the Stone Mountain Highland Games in 1977 Berthoff (1982) observed an audience comprising almost entirely of white people. "Evidently, Highland games now provide" he proposed, "an acceptable refuge from the courts and commissions that since 1954 have been ordering racial integration in public and quasi-private places" (Berthoff, 1982: p. 26). At this Stone Mountain Games, Berthoff met a Scottish-American man who had "joined the Scottish National Party on the supposition (quite mistaken) that, like the National Front in England, it seeks to keep blacks and Pakistanis out of Britain" (Berthoff, 1982: p. 26)[7].

Others assessing Scottish festivals in the US South have remarked upon a connection between Scottishness, Confederate nostalgia and whiteness. Focusing particularly on the state of Florida, Diane Roberts (1997; 1999a; 1999b) reports on the Tallahassee Scottish Highland Games and Celtic Festival. Following her visits to this event, which was inaugurated in 1996, Roberts (1997; 1999a; 1999b) concurs with the observation made by Berthoff (1982) at Stone Mountain. The people attending Scottish heritage events are predominantly, if not wholly, whites. Indeed, there are few, if any, non-white people at Highland Games, be these events in the American South or in the events held in the north-east that I observed during my own participation. Indeed, interviewee Jim Donaldson commented: "I suppose there are not many African-Americans though. One defining feature must be that most of those at the Games are white". Therefore, the issue of race and identity must be taken seriously as a critical aspect pertaining to the growth in interest in Scottish heritage since the 1970s.

Berthoff (1982) argues that by declaring oneself Scottish and reviving an ethnic association that one's ancestors may well have long forgotten, an individual is seeking "a defense against a society whose official commitment to equality of personal rights — to which he no doubt subscribes — has come to seem oddly oppressive to him" (Berthoff, 1982: p. 25). Such a reaction to contemporary society, Berthoff (1982: p. 25) contends, "bears a tinge of racism"[8]. In turn, Fry (1998: p. 19) contends that claims to Scottish ancestry in the American South, particularly in the post-Civil War period of the nineteenth century, existed "as a substitute for ... Confederate feeling". He proceeds to argue that in this mindset, "Somebody of Scottish descent was by definition not of black, Jewish, or other undesirable blood" (Fry, 1998: p. 19). Fry's contention reiterates Berthoff's (1982: p. 26) who, following his visit to Stone Mountain argued, "There may be black Macleans and Macleods, but they are tacitly assumed to have no properly Scottish ancestors and no place at Scottish-American gatherings" (Berthoff, 1982: p. 26).

Claiming that some Scottish-Americans believe non-white Scottish-Americans have "no properly Scottish ancestors" evokes a curious parallel with the opinions recounted by the British-born men I interviewed. As outlined above, these men said that other members within their Scottish-American community who attend Scottish heritage events do not have "real tie[s]" to Scotland and as a result they "pretend" they are Scottish. In much the same way, therefore, as Berthoff (1982) argues that some perceive white Scottish-Americans to be more 'authentically' Scottish than non-white Scottish-Americans, the men I spoke with identified those born in Scotland as 'authentic' Scots and others as "fanatics" with unconvincing claims to Scottishness. Depending on how ethno-national identity is defined, therefore, different subject positions accredit differing degrees of 'authenticity' and 'reality' to claims to Scottish ancestry and the identity substantiated therefrom.

At the Highland Games in Tallahassee, participants dress as Confederate soldiers and wear replica military uniforms of the short-lived nineteenth century state (Roberts, 1997; 1999a; 1999b). Noting the bagpipes playing Confederate songs, Roberts (1999a: p. 15) remarks: "Scotland is the embodiment of Old Dixie". Introducing Roberts's research to radio listeners, Liane Hansen explained that Highland Games in Florida have "more to do with the South than with Scotland" (in Roberts, 1997). Indeed, Roberts (1999b: p. 27) states: "It's not a big stretch to see Scotland morphing into a metaphor for the Old South". Ray (1998: p. 28) concurs, explaining there is a "mythic Scottish past that in the South blends harmoniously with nostalgic visions of an antebellum southern society and the Lost Cause". This conflation of Southern nostalgia for the Confederate States of America with a sense of Scottish heritage is exemplified by the appearance in 1997 of a Confederate memorial tartan (Ray, 1998; Sebesta, 2000).

Ray (1998) and Roberts (1999a; 1999b) concur that Confederate memorabilia and symbols are widely displayed and available at Scottish heritage events in the US South. Observing the Highlands and Islands Scottish Games and Celtic Festival in Biloxi, Mississippi, Ray (1998) records that many people attend wearing Confederate uniforms and singing Confederate songs. Yet, despite these clear displays of support for a briefly-existing nation-state whose raison d'être was to sustain slavery, Ray asserts that "Mourning the Old South's defeat or displaying the Confederate battle flag acquires *less problematic meanings* in the Scottish-heritage context" (Ray, 1998: p. 29; my emphasis). To justify this position, namely that support for the Confederate States of America and its white supremacist associations is somehow neutralised by people asserting their Scottish ancestry, Ray (1998: p. 29) offers this panacea: "The 'new southerner' involved in Scottish heritage is no longer just a white, Anglo southerner, but an ethnically Celtic southerner with other reasons for being different and unassailable justification for celebrating that difference" (Ray, 1998: p. 29). Excusing the Southern white Confederate associations on the "unassailable" basis of assuming those present are "ethnically Celtic" is a difficult contention to sustain. James (1999) shows that deeming anyone "Celtic" at the end of the twentieth century requires distortion of both the historical and archaeological records and a rather large leap of the imagination. Yet Ray (1998) argues that Scottish heritage in the South is merely an exuberant assertion of 'Celtic' ethnicity.

Ray's (1998: p. 29) sympathetic gaze over the South and its Scottish connections leads her to state that those attending Scottish games are expressing their Southern-Scottish identities in a manner that is "uncontroversial [and] multicultural". Yet this assurance that Scottish games are "uncontroversial [and] multicultural" is not matched by far-right political organisations whose recognition of an association between whiteness and Scottishness is encouraging them to attend Scottish heritage events in the United States[9].

The San Diego Scottish Games and Gathering of the Clans, held in Vista, California, has been an event in North America's Highland Games calendar since 1972. Held every June with an average attendance of around ten thousand (US Scots, 1996), it was targeted in 1998 by a neo-Nazi organisation with pamphlets praising "Aryan genius" and welcoming the Scottish Games as "one of the only places left in San Diego County where a WHITE person can gather with others of his or her own race in a peaceful and harmonious celebration of pride" (emphasis in original). A month later, in July 1998, the Virginia Scottish Games and Gathering of the Clans, held in Alexandria since 1974, was visited by the right wing organisation, the Council of Conservative Citizens. Members of this group distributed leaflets outlining their opposition to "Third World immigration". Reporting that their leaflets were "greatly received" by visitors to the Alexandria event, the organisation repeated the exercise at a Scottish heritage event in Maryland in July 1999 (*Citizens Informer*, 1998; 1999).

Held in Arlington since 1986, in 2001 the Texas Scottish Festival and Highland Games invited Grady McWhiney to present a speech about the American South as being both inherently 'Celtic' and violent. From 1994–2001 McWhiney was a director of the League of the South, a nationalist organization that hopes to revive the Confederate States of America (League of the South, 1999, 2000; SPLC, 2000). This group has recently been condemned as "clearly racist in its attitude toward black people" and is recognized as working with "other racist groups like the Council of Conservative Citizens" (SPLC, 2000: p. 29). Also in Texas, the Scottish heritage association the Scots of Austin pledged support in September 2000 for the Texas Heritage Coalition, an organisation that recognizes the removal of Confederate symbols from Texas as "nothing less than ethnic genocide of the Southern people and our culture" and compares the civil rights group the National Association for the Advancement of Colored People (NAACP) to the Nazis (Texas Heritage Coalition, 2001).

In sum, there is an emerging trend amongst far-right organizations in the United States to attend and distribute literature at Scottish festivals and Highland Games, particularly those in the American South. In return, a very small number of Scottish heritage associations whose members attend such events are independently acting to reciprocate by offering support, albeit symbolically, to these groups. This further challenges Ray's (1998: p. 29) assertion that Scottish heritage events are "multicultural" and is evidence of the way in which Scottish heritage can be appropriated and manipulated by some to construe pro-Confederate and white identities.

Conclusion

In the past thirty years there has been a rapid growth in the number and geographical distribution of Scottish heritage events in the United States. Much of this has occurred in the final five years of the twentieth century when, on average, fifteen new Scottish games and festivals were inaugurated annually. Yet within this booming production of Scottish heritage, my assessments reveal some contentions over the 'authenticity' of Scottish identity and connections to Scotland. These contrasting opinions are based on varying interpretations of how ethno-national identities are delineated. For some, having a Scottish birthplace is pertinent, for others, researching one's genealogy supports claims to Scottish ancestry. Further, and more worryingly, recent evidence suggests that in a few instances these Scottish heritage events are utilised by some to venerate the Confederate States of America (CSA) or proclaim a racialised white identity.

The interviews I conducted with participants at Highland Games in a north-eastern US state showed that many of those involved in hosting Scottish heritage events recognise them as stereotypical idealisations of Scotland. Yet many enjoy consuming and reproducing this clichéd image at Scottish festivals. If, as Ashworth (1994) argues, heritage is invested with meaning by consumers, both at individual and national scales, then the Scotland produced and consumed in the United States is as 'authentic' as any other. Yet is it an authentic Scotland being displayed or a vision of an authentic United States, particularly as the production and consumption of heritage is "central … to a nation's self-identity" (McCrone *et al.*, 1995: p. 14)? As a result, I suggest that Scottish heritage events in the United States are primarily about American nationality, albeit represented through a Scottish lens. Scottish heritage is a conduit through which to assess one's US nationality. A final example is illustrative. A few days before he attended a Scottish festival dressed as an eighteenth century Highlander James Donaldson told me, "American culture is struggling with the issues of national identity versus ethnicity". For him and many other Scottish-Americans, he explained, "Americanness is not quite enough".

Acknowledgements

I would like to thank Rosie Duncan and Rebecca Carlson for drawing the map.

Notes

1 In the 1990 census, under five percent of the three million US residents who claimed Scottish ethnicity were born outside the United States (US Census, 2000).

2 Although this paper focuses solely on examples from the United States, it is worth noting that there are Highland Games and Scottish heritage festivals all over the world, for example, in Canada, Australia, New Zealand and South Africa. Indeed, a Highland Games has been held in Jakarta, Indonesia since 1974 (Brander 1992, 1996).

3 Instances where the number of cases in the temporal data series is less than the corresponding number for the spatial data set is due to there being no inauguration date listed for the event concerned.

4 The Internet (1997) data set does not list inauguration dates. Consequently, events founded in the late-1990s appear only in Internet (2000). Thus, in the combined data set there are no inaugurations after 1996.

5 The Clan MacLachlan directory states the Milwaukee Highland Games and Scottish Festival at Glendale was established in 1835 (Internet, 2000), but the other data sources all consider this Wisconsin event to have begun around thirty years later in 1867.

6 The names of all interviewees are pseudonyms. Interviews were not recorded and hand-written notes were transcribed immediately following the interview.

7 The Neill Report on Standards in Public Life (1998) limited membership of British political parties to those eligible to vote in British elections. Thus, the individual encountered by Berthoff (1982) would now not be eligible to join the Scottish National Party.

8 Examining a Canadian example from Nova Scotia in the first half of the twentieth century, McKay (1992: p. 25) argues that a valourisation and romanticisation of Scottish heritage "intelligently and subtly ... [develops] a notion of racial essence". McKay (1992: p. 44) continues stating that in Nova Scotia, "racial hierarchies were quietly at work in tartanism".

9 The US organization most associated with white supremacy and racism is the Ku Klux Klan. Its connections to Scotland, and in particular it foundation by a group of Scottish-American Confederate veterans in the late-1860s, are widely documented. See, for example, Wade (1987), Hewitson (1993), Scott (1997), Hook (1997, 1999), Roberts (1999b), Seenan (1999), Hague (forthcoming).

References

ASGF (1995) *1995 Questionnaire results*. (Available from the Association of Scottish Games and Festivals. Available HTTP: http://www.asgf.org/)

Ashworth, G.J. (1994) 'From history to heritage: From heritage to identity: In search of concepts and models', in G. J. Ashworth and P. J. Larkham (eds) *Building a new heritage: Tourism, culture and identity in the new Europe*. London and New York: Routledge, pp. 13–30.

Ashworth, G.J. and Larkham, P.J. (eds) (1994) *Building a New Heritage: Tourism, culture and identity in the new Europe*. London and New York: Routledge.

Berthoff, R. (1982) 'Under the kilt: Variations on the Scottish-American ground', *Journal of American Ethnic History*, Vol. 1, No. 1: pp. 5–34.

Brander, M. (1992) *The essential guide to Highland Games*. Edinburgh: Canongate.

Brander, M. (1996) *The world directory of Scottish Associations*. Glasgow: Neil Wilson Publishing.

Citizens Informer (1998) 'Very active CofCC in DC area', 3rd Quarter, p.4.

———— (1999) 'National capital region CofCC', Summer, p.4.

Congressional Record: Senate (1998) 'National Tartan Day' (Text of Resolution). Congressional Record — Senate, Vol. 144: p. S2373.

Cornwell, Tim (2000) 'Roots, mon', *The Scotsman*, 12 March.

Donaldson, E. A. (1986) *The Scottish Highland Games in America*. Gretna: Pelican Publishing Company.

Fry, M. (1998) 'Plaid by the wrong rules', *The Herald*, 23 March, p.19.

Hague, E. (2000) 'Scotland on film: Attitudes and opinions about Braveheart', *Etudes Ecossiases*, No. 6, pp. 75–89.

Hague, E. (forthcoming) 'The Scottish Diaspora: Tartan Day and the appropriation of Scottish identities in the United States', in D. Harvey; R. Jones; N. McInroy and C. Milligan (eds) *Celtic geographies*. London: Routledge.

Hewison, R. (1987) *The heritage industry: Britain in a climate of decline*. London: Methuen.

Hewitson, J. (1993) *Tam Blake and Co.: The story of the Scots in America*. Edinburgh: Canongate.

Hook, A. (1997) 'They have taken over Hollywood's vision of a heroic Scotland', *The Herald*, 29 November: p. 17.

Hook, A. (1999) *From Goosecreek to Gandercleugh: Studies in Scottish-American literary and cultural theory*. East Linton: Tuckwell Press.

Hunter, J. (1997) 'How should we treat America's growing obsession with its Scottish connections?', *Scotland on Sunday*, 11 May: p. 17.

Internet (1997) The Gathering of the Clans — Clan Calendar. Source page — http://www.tartans.com/ Data downloaded from http://www.discribe.ca/cgi-bin/clancal.cgi/search/www/htdocs/clancal?country=USA (Site accessed August–September 1997)

Internet (2000) The Clan MacLachlan Association of North America, Inc. Source page — http://www.maclachlans.org/ Data downloaded from — http://www.maclachlans.org/internet/ONELINE.HTM (Site accessed April–May 2000)

James, S. (1999) *The Atlantic Celts: Ancient people or modern invention?* London: British Museum Press.

Jarvie, G. (1991) *Highland Games: The making of the myth*. Edinburgh: Edinburgh University Press.

Jarvie, G. (2000) 'Sport, the èmigré, and the dance called America', *Sport History Review*, Vol. 31, No. 1: pp. 28–42.

Kirshenblatt-Gimblett, B. (1998) *Destination culture: Tourism, museums, and heritage*. Berkeley, Los Angeles and London: University of California Press.

League of the South (1999) 'The League of the South National Board of Directors', Page downloaded from http://dixienet.org/ls-bod/board.html (Site accessed 2 August 1999).

League of the South (2000) 'League of the South Membership Application Page: The League of the South has a dream...', Page downloaded from — http://www.dixienet.org/ls-homepg/ls-appl.html (Site accessed 5 November 2000)

Linklater, A. (1998) 'Day the US wraps itself in tartan', *The Herald*, 6 April: p. 2.

McCrone, D., Morris, A., and Kiely, R. (1995) *Scotland — the brand: The making of Scottish heritage*. Edinburgh: Edinburgh University Press.

McKay, I. (1992) 'Tartanism triumphant: The construction of Scottishness in Nova Scotia, 1933–1954', *Acadiensis*, Vol. 21, No. 2, pp. 5–47.

Neill Report (1998) *5th Report of the Committee on Standards in Public Life: the funding of political parties in the United Kingdom* (2 vols). London: The Stationary Office.

Ray, C. (1998) 'Scottish heritage Southern style', *Southern Cultures*, Vol. 4, No. 2, pp. 28–45.

Roberts, D. (1997) 'Essay', *Weekend Edition*, 16 November. National Public Radio (USA). Transcript available from NPR, Burrelle's Transcripts, P.O.Box 7, Livingston, NJ07039-0077, USA.

Roberts, D. (1999a) 'Nostalgic Dixie whistles up a Scottish melody', *The Times*, 16 August: p. 15.

Roberts, D. (1999b) 'Your clan or ours?', *Oxford American*, No. 29: pp. 24–30.

Scott, K. (1997) 'The fatal attraction', *The Herald*, 6 August, p.12.

Sebesta, E. H. (2000) 'The Confederate memorial tartan — officially approved by the Scottish Tartan Authority', *Scottish Affairs*, No. 31: pp. 55–84.

Seenan, G. (1999) 'Klansmen take their lead from Scots', *The Guardian*, 30 January, p.12.

Shah, D. K. and Arthur, H. (1978) 'Scotland the South', *Newsweek*, July 24, pp. 88–89.

Southern Poverty Law Center (SPLC) (2000) *Intelligence report: Rebels with a cause, Issue 99*. (Available from: The Intelligence Project, SPLC, 400 Washington Avenue, Montgomery, AL36104, USA.)

Texas Heritage Coalition (2001) 'Declaration of Solidarity', Page downloaded from http://www.geocities.com/txhrco/index.html (Site accessed 3 April 2001).

Urry, J. (1990) *The tourist gaze: Leisure and travel in contemporary societies*. London: Sage.

US Census (2000) US Census Bureau. Source page — http://www.census.gov/ (Site accessed 20–31 May 2000)

US Scots (1996) *The 1996 Guide to Games and Festivals*. (Available from US Scots, PO Box 20217, Columbus, oh43220, USA.)

Wade, W. C. (1987) *The Firey Cross: The Ku Klux Klan in America*. New York and Oxford: Oxford University Press.

Wright: P. (1991 [1985]) *On living in an old country*. London: Verso.

Young, N. and Macfarlane, C. (1998) 'The day America will turn tartan', *Scotland on Sunday*, 22 March: p. 7.

Visiting Places with 'Added Value': Learning from Pilgrimage to Enhance the Visitor's Experience at Heritage Attractions

Angela Phelps

Department of International Studies, Nottingham Trent University

Introduction

In an increasingly competitive leisure market, all attractions are seeking ways to develop visitor satisfaction, recognising that good quality 'customer care' is the best way to encourage both new and repeat visitors (Leask and Yeoman, 1999). In the last year the number of visits being made to heritage attractions has become more than a matter of academic debate or commercial interest. The continuing public argument in the UK concerning some of the more celebrated projects funded by the Millennium Commission has resulted in politicians and journalists grappling with patterns of visitor flow. While it is clear that inflated targets have led to unreasonable accusations of failure, it is equally clear that the total number of visits being made each year has been in decline over recent years (Middleton, 1990; Black, 2000; Mori, 2001). This is an important finding, with far-reaching significance. With more Millennium Commission funded projects still to open, how will existing attractions compete?

Extending the commercialism of an attraction is an obvious response to falling revenue, designed to encourage more visitors and increase the spend-per-head. However, heritage attractions are caught in a dilemma: by their very nature there is potential conflict between access and conservation. Too many visitors may result in negative impact on both the quality of the visitor experience and the conservation of the resource. Too much emphasis on commercial income may undermine heritage messages based on conservation and education values. What is required is a sustainable audience, one that is predictable in size and seasonal flow, to provide a reliable visitor income that may be fed into the long-term conservation plans of a site. Many mission statements for heritage attractions put responsibility towards the heritage resource first, and their visitors second. This is understandable given the conservation ethic prompting interest in such sites, but it may be problematic if it goes as far as to suggest disinterest in visitors. It is important to recognise that long-term conservation aims can only be achieved with viable financial planning, and in many cases that includes substantial, and reliable, income from visitors. An interesting finding in Richard Prentice's summaries of visitor research at heritage attractions is that, with the exception of city based museums and galleries, many heritage attractions do not have a significant proportion of repeat visitors amongst their audience (Prentice, 1989). However, this research pays little attention to location. Heritage centres in well-developed tourism areas benefit from a continually renewed audience and may not need to worry about what proportion of these visitors will return; heritage centres not favoured by tourism development depend for their long term survival on encouraging a steady flow of repeat visiting by local people. This means that the experience must be both memorable and enjoyable, and offer opportunities for different types of engagement. Market research repeatedly demonstrates that the most effective form of advertising is positive 'word of mouth'. Attractions need to provide a good experience for their visitors, not just to encourage existing visitors to come back, but to ensure they report well to their friends and family.

This paper addresses the presentation at new heritage attractions: can this be heightened in ways that will improve visitor experience, without impacting negatively on the resource? A comparison is made with what may be described as the longest standing heritage attractions: pilgrimage sites. In seeking to understand the distinctiveness offered by a visit to a heritage attraction the experience of pilgrimage is persuasive. Religious shrines have developed large and sustainable audiences, sometimes stretching over centuries. Also they have an extraordinary geographical reach, some drawing on a catchment spanning continents, with well-marked pilgrimage pathways supported by significant infrastructure. Such sites exist in semi-formalised hierarchies of global, national and local significance, meeting the needs of a segregated market. Pilgrimage sites demonstrate incredible market success, with massive drawing power for both new and repeat business. What, if anything, can the new heritage attractions learn about visitor experience from the process of pilgrimage?

For this paper a heritage attraction is defined as a site open to visitors, but where the long term aim is to conserve and protect the basic components providing the heritage value: buildings and monuments, objects, landscape or wildlife. Three examples of heritage attractions in the UK are used to explore aspects of the visitor experience: a conservation trust industrial site, a volunteer run transport attraction and a privately operating country house. Comparison will be made with both the process of pilgrimage and the nature of a pilgrimage site. Pilgrimage sites are distinctive in terms of the experience of a visit, as their whole existence rests on the deep personal significance drawn from being in a venerated place. Secular sites may also become so important culturally that they go through a parallel process of identification. Dean MacCannell suggests that international tourist 'sights' emerge by staged naming, framing and reproduction:

This miracle of consensus that transcends national boundaries rests on an elaborate set of institutional mechanisms, a twofold process of sight sacralization that is met with a corresponding ritual attitude on the part of the tourists. (1976: p. 42)

Kenneth Foote discusses how sites marked by tragedy or violence also become sanctified by ritual, memorial and periodic remembrance activities (Foote, K. 1997). Heritage sites open as visitor attractions may be able to enhance such inner meaning to intensify the experience of their visitors. This paper will focus on two aspects of pilgrimage, respect for the site and construction of the experience as reflected in the concept of a personal journey.

Learning from pilgrimage

Many heritage attractions aspire to both the large catchment and the place within the global hierarchy enjoyed by traditional religious pilgrimage sites. Despite their secular nature, there are parallels in the conviction of many managers concerning the intrinsic values embedded in the places in their care; the challenge is to find ways to convey this sense of place, and the special values attached to the buildings and objects, to visitors with no prior knowledge of the site. These may not be religious values, but they are still of great cultural significance. The shrines that provide the focus of pilgrimage activity are treated with great respect — a respect that influences the way they are visited, if not always including the nature of the on-site presentation. Religious shrines have an intrinsic attraction built within specific belief systems, so suggestions of connections with the hedonism of much modern tourism can provoke outrage. Pilgrims are perceived as people set apart by their devotion, and the process of pilgrimage separates them from the soullessness of the tourism journey (Cohen, E. 1992). Deconstructing the process of pilgrimage may identify elements that could usefully be adopted and adapted by other heritage attractions to help enhance the quality of their visitors' experience.

Pilgrimage has been written about for almost as long as it has existed as a recognisable activity. Some of the earliest texts definable as travel guides were written to ease the path of pilgrims. More recently theologians, philosophers, sociologists, geographers and others in many branches of the humanities and cultural studies have observed and engaged in pilgrimage in an attempt to establish the special qualities that sustain the activity. A number of recurrent themes mediate the relationship of three essential elements: the pilgrim, the pilgrimage and the shrine:

- the pilgrim is an intrinsically motivated person, expecting inner development through visiting a specific destination;
- the pilgrimage is a purposeful journey — both the process of the journey and arrival at the destination are planned and conducted according to rituals designed to extract the greatest personal meaning;

- the shrine is a unique destination — there may be many shrines, but each has a specific meaning that can only be appreciated fully by literally taking place. The pilgrim places his or her body as close as possible to the object of their attraction.

The emergent themes are the liminality of the experience, and the respect shown to the path and the destination (Turner and Turner, 1978). Pilgrims are seen as detached from both their own normal existence and the normal lives they encounter on the journey. Such detachment is prompted by a strong intrinsic motivation for making the journey. Pilgrimage presents a distinct category of visiting, as the quality of the experience will be heavily influenced by a long planning period, in which the pilgrim makes personal preparation for both the journey and its expected outcome. This contrasts with visits to international tourist attractions, which follow publicly prescribed paths allowing little individual selection: "modern international sightseeing possesses its own moral structure, a collective sense that certain sights must be seen" (MacCannell, 1976: p. 42). This may account for the lack of engagement frequently observed in the tourist progress, where visitors stream past the sights, rarely stopping longer than the time necessary to take a photograph. Such evidence as exists on motivation suggests that most leisure day-visits are spontaneous, rarely planned more than a day ahead of the event. Managers of heritage attractions could learn from this, and make more effort to encourage individual motivation and pre-visit planning; this may act to enhance personal engagement in a visit and generate more lasting memories.

The pilgrimage has been described as a ritualistic journey, with phases recognised by both participants and observers. These phases fall into four main groups:
- 'awakening': the longing or call, and departure — pilgrims are knowledgeable travellers, who will have prepared for a specific experience;
- 'ordeal': the path or labyrinth — this separates the pilgrim from their normal life, and impedes their progress by real, or imaginary, obstacles to be overcome, enhancing the achievement of reaching the destination;
- 'arrival': finding self — the emotional investment in the concept of arrival creates an experience offering the highest levels of self-actualisation, outweighing the extrinsic values of the site observed by casual visitors;
- 'return' — bringing back a boon, reintegration into society with added status.

These stages can be identified in the leisure visit, although with less definition. Leisure visits require motivation, both to make the trip and select a destination. Although the basic definition of leisure will dictate a pleasurable experience, there may still be hurdles to overcome — to check opening times, book tickets and arrange the journey. The visitors themselves may make little effort to mark arrival, but there is increasing recognition by managers of the importance of the welcome extended. There is also a clear parallel in the return with memory, aided by photographs and souvenirs. A distinguishing characteristic is that pilgrims seek something experiential, and often leave a personal statement, as opposed to tourists who frequently travel without purpose and take mementos. This is also shown in the observation that pilgrims travel towards their goal, while tourism is frequently described as providing escape.

Judith Adler has discussed the origins of sightseeing, and drew attention to aspects that could be related to pilgrimage (Adler, 1989). Conducting a visit is seen as movement through a culturally conceived space, with deliberate acts intended to reveal meaning, including the process of projecting the body through space. Her argument shows very readily how meanings are constructed, so that the modern visitor may occupy the same space as visitors in the past, but experience the places in quite different ways. Tim Edensor identifies the processes producing both pilgrimage and tourism spaces, which entail controlled access, surveillance and orchestrated activities (Edensor, 1998). A distinction is found only in the types of activity considered appropriate.

Heritage attractions are defined as such by their association with buildings, collections and events that have meaning beyond the aesthetic, due to their social, cultural and political context. Just as in the religious pilgrimage sites, it is these meanings that 'add value' and, if conveyed to visitors successfully, are reflected in both the respect shown to the site and the personalised quality of the visit experience. Managers of heritage attractions need to enhance both aspects, as respect for the site under-pins conservation and a good quality experience will encourage repeat visiting. Every age has renewed shrines and produced new places of pilgrimage — places associated with holy people, spiritual power and significant events. Tim Edensor recognises that representation is an integral part of the production of such places, so that symbolic sites may be consumed in different contexts: "places have multiple identities, (they) are situated points at which a variety of activities occur and a diverse range of people pass through on different routes" (Edensor, 1998: p. 20). The processes that 'add value' to the visit to a shrine may contain features that are transferable to enhance and deepen other types of visit experience. The challenge is to accommodate the variety of motivation, creating the opportunity for casual visitors to engage in more meaningful encounters.

Understanding the visitor experience: three examples

The description of a visit to a heritage site identified with a past industrial process will be used to explore the respect that can be engendered by a secular site. Geevor Tin Mine is one of a number of important derelict industrial locations in Cornwall. A working tin mine for centuries, it only ceased production in 1991 when the fall in commodity prices finally rendered it uneconomic. This timing is significant as it is sufficiently recent that much physically survives, including many of the people who worked there. The mine has become a symbol of the loss of industrial jobs that has undermined the economy of southwest Cornwall, and was marked as such even when it was still open, by a workers' demonstration against closure in London in the 1980's. Another important factor is that the mine became redundant well after a significant shift in attitude towards the importance of industrial heritage had occurred in the UK (Buchanan, 1980; Alfrey and Putnam, 1992). Even before production ceased, there was a clear intention to mark the site, not erase it from the landscape. The site is now managed by the Trevithick Trust[1], as part of a long-term scheme to save and present the heritage of the industrial revolution.

At the 'Geevor Experience' the visitor is offered a self-guided trail incorporating a museum and the surface workshops, and a guided mine visit. The trail starts in the museum, much of which features the recent past, presented in a traditional glass case arrangement of relics, with explanation of mineralisation and the mining process. Pictures and videos tell the story of efforts to save the mining industry, but still largely focused on the mining process and economic reasons for closure. Many faces appear, but without personal details or context. The mine workshops are presented almost as left on the day of closure, with little explanation of the derelict equipment to be seen; the trail continues through the ore processing plant, but with no working machinery and little interpretation. However, the visit takes a completely different turn, both in theme and style, when visitors embark on a guided walk through a 300 year old adit mine. When the site first opened as a heritage centre the visitor was offered a trip deep underground, in the most recently worked seams stretching out under the sea. After production ceased, the pumps were not maintained and these workings gradually flooded. These visits had to cease on grounds of health and safety. In an attempt to retain the attractiveness of the site the managers substituted a walk through a much older adit mine, which remains dry and well supported (although modern bracing and lighting have been added).

The underground tour is conducted by interpreters, some of whom once worked in the mine. With limited props, the guide brings the narrow and claustrophobic tunnel to life by focusing on the working day of an eighteenth century miner and the children who would have assisted him. For the first time in the visit, the visitors are prompted to empathise — with the assistance of the cold, damp, cramped, dark conditions visitors are invited to consider what it felt like to work there. Questions and answers cover the mining process, the effort involved, the product and the effect of the activity on the health and welfare of the miners; personal experience is used to compare the miner's life in the eighteenth century with the most recent experience before closure. In 15 minutes the mine comes alive, and visitors emerge into the bright light not nostalgic for a romanticised golden age, but profoundly respectful for the people who survived such austere conditions, and perhaps a little thankful that such times have past.

This example illustrates a common problem — the difficulty of engaging casual visitors with the special characteristics of a heritage attraction. The difficulty is marked by the different reaction of visitors to the interpretation offered. The most powerful engagement came right at the end of the visit. This is valuable in that it gives a strong finish to the visit, but it could have been used as a more effective introduction, to set a context for the museum treatment of the modern period. There is a visible change in the response of the visitors to the last element of the Geevor Experience, to a degree that reflects more than just the change to live interpretation. The experience gained in the adit mine captures something of the 'specialness' of this site: this contributed the 'added value' that defines a heritage visit.

The layout of this trail reflects another common problem, particularly noticeable on sites protected by conservation charities and run by enthusiastic volunteers. The focus is on the buildings and the objects in the collection. There seems to be little consideration of the experience of a visitor, particularly one with no knowledge of the subject matter at the outset. On such sites the buildings and objects attract enormous respect from knowledgeable volunteers, but in a way that isolates the non-participant visitor. The presentation could be enhanced by finding ways to convey the reasons for that respect to the visitor more effectively. Although the work experience of some volunteers 'adds value', a more effective long-term strategy would be to record their experience and use this to enhance the interpretation throughout the experience.

The problems encountered in attempting to accommodate different types of visitors are demonstrated most clearly at special interest sites. Visitor survey work conducted at the second example, Nottingham Transport Heritage Centre, identified a clear division in the audience between the special interest visitors and family visitors seeking an enjoyable day out. The venture is run entirely by volunteers, making it a significant leisure activity in itself, before any visitors arrive. The Centre is the home of three transport groups: the Great Central Railway (Northern Development Association), the Midland Society of Model and Experimental Engineers and a group of bus enthusiasts restoring vintage service buses. These three transport interests share a site within Rushcliffe Country Park, which was established in 1994 using a derelict land reclamation grant on the former Ordnance Depot adjoining Ruddington, a village 4 miles south of Nottingham. The Transport Heritage Centre is open to the public on Sundays and Bank Holiday Mondays from Easter to October, when the members operate a steam railway, vintage bus rides and three gauges of model railway with steam and diesel traction. Volunteers also staff a shop, café, bric-a-brac and 'cinema' coach in which videos of vintage transport are shown.

A visitor survey was conducted in the 1998 season to establish the market profile of the visitors and to investigate their motivation[2]. A sample of visitors was drawn from 5 days, representing normal Sunday opening, Bank Holidays and one Saturday for a special event. This covered the range of operation when visitors were charged to go into the site, and provided a sample of 157 visiting groups. The results show that the Centre operates as a local and regional leisure attraction, as well as a national special interest attraction. The total catchment is wide but the focus is highly concentrated: the majority of the groups had travelled less than 30 miles (see Figure 1, page following). Most of the visiting groups could be considered 'special interest' as at least one person

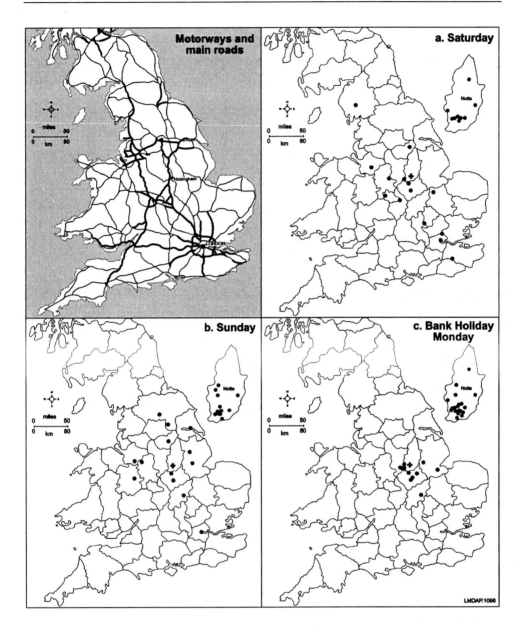

Figure 1   Nottingham Transport Heritage Centre:
origin of visitors, sample survey 1998

in the group expressed an interest in transport heritage. However, many of these visitors also said they were on a 'general day out'. This reflects a further complication in trying to identify segments in an audience: mixed motivation may be found within one group.

Most of the visitors arrived by car, but there was a significant increase in bus travel on the day of the special event, which was a bus gala. Some of the visitors arriving by bus had travelled to Nottingham by train, including visitors from Doncaster, Uttoxeter and Manchester. These visitors are not simply 'meandering' (Cheshire and Stabler, 1976), but were special interest visitors making a pilgrim's progress involving several modes of transport to enhance their enjoyment of the experience. A third of the visitors had been to the Nottingham Transport Heritage Centre on a previous occasion. The largest proportion of first time visitors came on the special event day, with the normal Sundays showing the highest proportion of returning visitors. More than two thirds of the family groups were on their first visit, whist more than half of those returning were adult-only groups. The site offers little interpretation, so it is not surprising that the majority of the returning visitors are knowledgeable transport enthusiasts. As several visitors reported, one of the attractions was watching the progress being made. On this evidence, the site is not succeeding in persuading the 'general day out' family visitors to return.

Most visitors came in groups of three or more, but nearly a fifth came alone. The family groups are most frequent on the normal Sunday opening and the proportion increases significantly for the Bank Holiday days. There is a marked increase in the proportion of individual visitors on the special event day. Thus more single people, in this case often men, will travel to visit when there is a particular event of interest to them. This produces an unusually high proportion of single visitors in comparison with many other attractions, reflecting the 'special interest' character of the audience. Nevertheless, most visitors came in family groups, of mixed ages and gender. Although a third of the visitors were children under 12 this is a lower proportion than many museums and heritage centres attract, again reflecting the higher proportion of adults amongst the 'special interest' audience. A significantly higher proportion of the visitors with children were on general days out, whereas most of the adult-only parties had a special interest in transport.

There is clear evidence that the Nottingham Heritage Centre is attracting two distinct visiting groups. The visitors with a special interest in transport heritage are predominantly adults, and are prepared to travel quite long distances for a day-trip. There is a greater likelihood that they will visit alone or with one other person, and they are more likely to visit for a special event. The second type of visitor group comprises people on general leisure half day-trips. They travel shorter distances and are more likely to bring children. These visitors are found in greater proportion on the normal open days and Bank Holidays. This example demonstrates the variability of an audience. The special interest visitor displays many of the attributes of a pilgrim, in terms of preparation, knowledge of the site, the importance of the journey to the site and reverence shown to the objects on display. The volunteers running the site recognise this type of visitor in themselves and without question steer the presentation to cater for them: they expect visitors to share their interest in transport. However, catering exclusively for such visitors may result in a potentially more numerous audience of general visitors being ignored. These differences need to be recognised at all stages of the process of a visit. Whereas special interest visitors may have a pilgrim's foreknowledge and recognition of key artefacts, general day out visitors seek entertainment and need to be offered an enjoyable way into understanding the special characteristics of the site.

The final example has been chosen to demonstrate how a visit may be constructed to meet a specific need, but in doing so may restrict the attractiveness of a site. Althorp House in Northamptonshire offers a pilgrimage to a shrine created for Diana, Princess of Wales. Charles (9th Earl) Spencer describes in his book about Althorp House the remodelling of the day visit after the death of his sister. In many respects the visit now offers the classic pilgrimage elements. The presentation of the site emphasises the association of the place with a person who, if not holy, was certainly special. The place association with Princess Diana in life is tenuous, but the association with death, as the proclaimed burial site, is undeniable. The graveside visit is perhaps the most accessible, and replicated, pilgrimage. Graves and cemeteries are sites awash with special feelings due to their function in protecting bodily remains. In many ways they offer an opportunity to touch, and be touched, by occupying a space associated with the body of the person venerated or remembered. The poignancy of many memorials not associated with burial is the absence of the body (Phelps, 1998).

At Althorp the visitors voluntarily, and apparently enthusiastically, enter into the process of pilgrimage. It is necessary to book, and therefore the visit must be planned well in advance of the event. As constructed, this visit is not spontaneous so is more likely to be engaged in thoughtfully. A limit of 2,500 tickets a day was a deliberate policy set when the site opened in 1998 to restrict the number of visitors. Althorp is only open for a 60-day season, in respect of tax relief on treasures held. By disturbing co-incidence the dates agreed for the season prior to Princess Diana's death stretch from her birthday, 1st July, to just before the date of her death on 31st August. Whilst conserving the site by preventing crowds these restrictions also serve to accentuate the 'special' status of a visit.

The pilgrimage path functions to slow the pilgrim down, creating detachment from the everyday and space to focus on the purpose of the journey. Althorp is not easy to reach even by car, and once there much walking is involved in the visit. The car park is remote from the house, outside the main gate. Although transport to the visitor centre is offered, many visitors choose to walk up the drive following a marked path to the start of a carefully controlled visit at the entrance to the converted stable block. The visitor negotiates a trail of attractions in the courtyard café, museum and house before being released into the park to walk to the burial site. The museum is laid out as a selective progress through the life of the Princess, culminating not in her death, but the bizarre 'life after death' of her clothing, displayed in a street scene of shop windows, into which visitors gaze as they pass by. The approach to the shrine is carefully orchestrated. A winding path through wooded parkland gradually reveals the lake, the island and the shrine. The focus of attention is a constructed shrine, not the burial site that remains inaccessible on the island. Visitors queue quietly to place flowers and take photographs, notably a marker picture of themselves with their back to the shrine — placing themselves by association. The return path includes the shop, curiously presented in similar mode to the museum. Objects are displayed behind glass, mounted, lit and labelled. On request replicas may be purchased, encased within purple wrappings, to be carried back along the processional route as symbols of the visit.

This site works for the people who want to venerate Diana; the degree of preparation involved mean those who don't want to engage in this way will simply stay away. The gentle progress slows the visitor in a way that leads to detachment from the usual noise of a leisure visit, leaving space for contemplation and reflection. How long the site will work in this respect is questionable; the enhanced marketing activities noticeable recently suggest interest is already waning. However, the presentation of the visit could be changed if it ceases to meet the needs of visitors in the future. Here the pilgrim's progress is prioritised in a way that creates a build-up to the revelation of the shrine as the focus for the visit. Again, the key underpinning quality is respect, but the visit is constructed in a way that encourages visitors to engage in personal reflection.

The importance of visitor satisfaction in encouraging repeat visits

If visitors are to be encouraged to repeat their activity, whether at the same site or at a succession of similar sites, a good experience needs to be assured. Consideration of pilgrimage sites suggests an approach that can 'add value' through enhanced engagement. "Travellers cannot find deep meaning in their journey until they encounter what is truly sacred" (Cousineau, 1998: p. xxviii). But sacred does not just mean holy, it can also mean something that is worthy of reverence, evoking wonder and awe. Heritage attractions have an enormous advantage over the more commercial tourism attractions in that they can exploit the contemplation of the heritage resources in their care to 'add value' to a visit. In his study of visitors to the Taj Mahal, Tim Edensor encountered religious pilgrims alongside domestic and international tourists. An interesting observation was the dissonance between these groups. Western tourists were predominantly focused on visual consumption, venerating the aesthetic qualities of the site and attempting to achieve the isolation of Urry's romantic gaze, even when visiting in rushed package tour groups. They criticised the apparently less reverent bustle created by the domestic visitors, not recognising the importance of group interaction experienced by religious pilgrims more interested in placing themselves in a spiritual location than contemplating a beautiful sight.

Conclusion

The parallel of pilgrimage offers one approach to exploring qualities that can add value for secular visitors. The recurrent themes are respect for the site and the role of detachment and engagement created through the process of a visit. Pilgrims achieve considerable involvement — they are curious, aware and responsive. They achieve a degree of self-actualisation that makes the experience profoundly memorable, if not addictive. These are responses that could be enhanced to add value to any visit. The key is the degree of empathy developed; respect for the resource can be encouraged by slowing the process of a visit to allow people time for reflection. A realisation drawn from many heritage attractions, is that an essential quality of the visit is conveyed by the successful interpretation of social history, prompting empathy between a visitor and the people who occupied the places visited in past times. This empathy produces a respect for the site transferable into the current visit. It is important to recognise the variety of people found in any audience and not just present a site to those already receptive to the message. Interpretation that encourages reflection and personal involvement offers a degree of engagement that makes a visit memorable.

Despite suggestions of a collapse of heritage visiting, and a dearth of repeat visitors, there is a great deal of repeat visiting going on. However, this only becomes apparent if you stand back from the individual attraction and consider the wider picture. Heritage visitors do repeat the 'heritage visit experience' — perhaps as much as once a week in the summer. However, they are visiting a succession of different heritage attractions. Audience research is usually focused on one site and as such, may obscure the wider picture. The development of a competitive market is counter-productive for heritage attractions. These would do better to work together towards a common conservation aim, with the support of a common sustainable audience. All heritage attractions share an opportunity and a responsibility towards developing that audience, but it may be difficult to appreciate this from one site, as the result of successful visit is likely to be a repeat 'heritage' visit elsewhere. Greater attention to aspects of presentation that encourage preparation and empathy should result in visitors addicted to the process of visiting heritage attractions, creating a pool of repeating visitors for all heritage attractions to draw on.

Notes

1   "The Trevithick Trust is an educational trust and charity, running and managing industrial heritage sites across Cornwall. Formed in 1993, it takes its name from the acclaimed engineer Richard Trevithick (1771–1833), who was born near Camborne. Its aim is to preserve Cornish industrial heritage sites for future generations in a way which makes them informative and interesting for visitors. Trevithick Trust's research presents you with an authentic experience of life during the industrial revolution in Cornwall. There's something for everyone, from tin mines to a china clay museum, from the picturesque thatched cottage where Richard Trevithick lived to lonely lighthouses in breathtaking settings." (Trust Leaflet, 2000)

2   This survey would not have been possible without the active involvement of volunteers on the site; particular thanks are extended to Mr Alan Kemp for distributing questionnaires at the gate.

References

Adler, J. (1989) 'Origins of sightseeing', *Annals of Tourism Research* Vol. 16, No. 1: pp. 7–29.

Alfrey, J. and Putnam, T. (1992) *The industrial heritage: Managing resources and use.* London: Routledge.

Black, G. (2000) 'Perspectives on visitors', *Lottery Monitor* Vol. 4, Issue 8: pp. 14–15.

Buchanan, R.A. (1980) *Industrial archaeology in Britain.* London: Allen Lane.

Cohen, E. (1992) 'Pilgrimage centres: Concentric and excentric', *Annals of Tourism Research* Vol. 19, No. 1: pp. 33–50.

Cousineau, P. (1999) *The art of pilgrimage.* Shaftesbury, Dorset: Element.

Cheshire, P.C. and Stabler, M.J. (1976) 'Joint consumption benefits in recreational site "surplus": An empirical estimate', *Regional Studies* Vol. 10, No. 4: pp. 343–51.

Edensor, T. (1998) Tourists at the Taj: performance and meaning at a symbolic site London and New York: Routledge.

Foote, K. (1997) *Shadowed ground: America's landscapes of violence and tragedy.* Austin: University of Texas Press.

Leask, A. and Yeoman, I. (eds.) (1999) *Heritage visitor attractions: An operations management perspective.* London: Cassell.

MacCannell, D. (1976) *The tourist: A new theory of the leisure class.* London: Macmillan.

Middleton, V. (1990) *New vision for independent museums in the UK.* London: Association of Independent Museums.

Mori (2001) *Visitors to museums and galleries in the UK.* Research study conducted for Resource: The Council for Museums, Archives and Libraries.

Phelps, A. (1998) 'Memorials without location: creating heritage places', *Area* Vol. 30, No. 2: pp 166–168.

Prentice, R. (1989) 'Visitors to heritage sites: A market segmentation by visitor characteristics', in D. T. Herbert, R. C. Prentice and C. J. Thomas (eds) *Heritage sites: Strategies for marketing and development*. Aldershot: Avebury, pp. 15–61.

Spencer, C. (1998) *Althorp: The story of an English house*. London: Viking.

Turner, V. and Turner, E. (1978) *Image and pilgrimage in christian culture*. Oxford: Blackwell.

Urry, J. (1995) *Consuming places*. London: Routledge.

Leisure Studies Association
LSA Publications

LSA

An extensive list of publications on a wide range of leisure studies topics, produced by the Leisure Studies Association since the late 1970s, is available from LSA Publications.

Some recently published volumes are detailed on the following pages, and full information may be obtained on newer and forthcoming LSA volumes from:

LSA Publications, c/o M. McFee
email: mcfee@solutions-inc.co.uk
The Chelsea School, University of Brighton
Eastbourne BN20 7SP (UK)
fax: (+44) (0)1323 644641

Among other benefits, members of the Leisure Studies Association may purchase LSA Publications at highly preferential rates.

Please contact LSA at the above address for information regarding membership of the Association, LSA Conferences, and LSA Newsletters.

LEISURE AND SOCIAL INCLUSION:
NEW CHALLENGES FOR POLICY AND PROVISION

**LSA Publication No. 73. ISBN: 0 906337 84 4 [2001] pp. 204
eds. Gayle McPherson and Malcolm Reid**

Contents

JUST LEISURE: EQUITY, SOCIAL EXCLUSION AND IDENTITY

LSA Publication No 72. ISBN: 0 906337 83 6 [2000] pp. 195+xiv
Edited by Celia Brackenridge, David Howe and Fiona Jordan

Contents

JUST LEISURE: POLICY, ETHICS AND PROFESSIONALISM

LSA Publication No 71. ISBN: 0 906337 81 X [2000] pp. 257+xiv
Edited by Celia Brackenridge, David Howe and Fiona Jordan

Contents

TOURISM AND VISITOR ATTRACTIONS: LEISURE, CULTURE AND COMMERCE

LSA Publication No 61. ISBN: 0 906337 71 2 [1998] pp. 211

Edited by Neil Ravenscroft, Deborah Philips and Marion Bennett

Contents

THE PRODUCTION AND CONSUMPTION OF SPORT CULTURES: LEISURE, CULTURE AND COMMERCE

LSA Publication No. 62. ISBN: 0 906337 72 0 [1998] pp. 178
Edited by Udo Merkel, Gill Lines, Ian McDonald

Contents

GENDER, SPACE AND IDENTITY:
LEISURE, CULTURE AND COMMERCE

LSA Publication No. 63. ISBN: 0 906337 73 9 [1998] pp. 191
Edited by Cara Aitchison and Fiona Jordan

Contents

CONSUMPTION AND PARTICIPATION: LEISURE, CULTURE AND COMMERCE

LSA Publication No. 64. ISBN: 0 906337 74 7 [2000]
Edited by Garry Whannel

Contents

POLICY AND PUBLICS

LSA Publication No. 65. ISBN: 0 906337 75 5 [1999] pp. 167
Edited by Peter Bramham and Wilf Murphy

Contents

LEISURE, TOURISM AND ENVIRONMENT (I)
SUSTAINABILITY AND ENVIRONMENTAL POLICIES

LSA Publication No. 50 Part I;
Edited by Malcolm Foley, David McGillivray and Gayle McPherson (1999);
ISBN 0 906337 64 X

Contents

LEISURE, TOURISM AND ENVIRONMENT (II)
PARTICIPATION, PERCEPTIONS AND PREFERENCES

LSA Publication No. 50 (Part II)
Edited by Malcolm Foley, Matt Frew and Gayle McPherson
ISBN: 0 906337 69 0; pp. 177+xii

Contents

LEISURE: MODERNITY, POSTMODERNITY AND LIFESTYLES

LSA Publications No. 48 (LEISURE IN DIFFERENT WORLDS Volume I)
Edited by Ian Henry (1994); ISBN: 0 906337   52 6, pp. 375+

Contents

(continued)

LEISURE, TIME AND SPACE: MEANINGS AND VALUES IN PEOPLE'S LIVES

LSA Publication No. 57. ISBN: 0 906337 68 2 [1998] pp. 198 + IV
Edited by Sheila Scraton

Contents